SCRIPTURE, THE SOUL OF THEOLOGY

Joseph A. Fitzmyer, S.J.

PAULIST PRESS
New York / Mahwah, NJ
1994

IMPRIMI POTEST
Rev. Edward Glynn, S.J.
Praepositus Provinciae Marylandiae

NIHIL OBSTAT
Rev. Stephen F. Brett, S.S.J.
Censor Deputatus

IMPRIMATUR
Reverend Msgr. William J. Kane
Vicar General for the Archdiocese of Washington
November 29, 1993

The *nihil obstat* and *imprimatur* are official declarations that a book or pamphlet is free of doctrinal or moral error. No implication is contained therein that those who have granted the *nihil obstat* and the *imprimatur* agree with the content, opinions, or statements expressed.

Library of Congress Cataloging-in-Publication Data

Fitzmyer, Joseph A.
    Scripture, the soul of theology/Joseph A. Fitzmyer.
    p. cm.
    Includes bibliographical references and indexes.
    ISBN 0-8091-3509-4 (pbk.)
    1. Bible—Hermeneutics. 2. Bible—Criticism, interpretation, etc.—History—19th century. 3. Bible—Criticism, interpretation, etc.—History—20th century. 4. Bible—Study—Catholic Church. 5. Bible and Christian union. 6. Catholic Church—Doctrines. I. Title.
    BS476.F58 1994
    220.6′01—dc20   94-15539

Published by Paulist Press
997 Macarthur Boulevard
Mahwah, NJ 07430

Printed and bound in the United States of America

CONTENTS

Sacrae autem Scripturae verbum Dei continent et, quia inspiratae, vere verbum Dei sunt; ideoque Sacrae Paginae studium sit veluti anima Sacrae Theologiae.

    (*Dei verbum* §24)

The Sacred Scriptures contain the Word of God and, since they are inspired, are indeed the Word of God; and so the study of the Sacred Page should be, as it were, the soul of sacred theology.

    (*Dogmatic Constitution on Divine Revelation* §24)

To
THE REVEREND RAYMOND E. BROWN, S.S.,
Indefatigable Interpreter of the Sacred Page
and Staunch Defender of the
Historical-Critical Method of Biblical Interpretation

ABBREVIATIONS

AAS	*Acta Apostolicae Sedis*
AB	*Anchor Bible*
ASS	*Acta Sanctae Sedis*
CBQ	*Catholic Biblical Quarterly*
CCLat	Corpus Christianorum, Latin Series
CSEL	Corpus scriptorum ecclesiasticorum latinorum
DS	H. Denzinger and A. Schönmetzer, *Enchiridion symbolorum* (32d ed.; Freiburg im B.: Herder, 1963)
EB	*Enchiridion biblicum* (4th ed.; Naples: M. D'Auria, 1961)
Exp Tim	*Expository Times*
GCS	Griechische christliche Schriftsteller
HTR	*Harvard Theological Review*
IDB	G. A. Buttrick (ed.), *The Interpreter's Dictionary of the Bible* (4 vols.; Nashville, TN: Abingdon, 1962)
IDBSup	K. Crim (ed.), *The Interpreter's Dictionary of the Bible, Supplementary Volume* (Nashville, TN: Abingdon, 1976)
IKZ	*Internationale kirchliche Zeitschrift*
JBL	*Journal of Biblical Literature*
KlT	Kleine Texte
NJBC	R. E. Brown et al. (eds.), *The New Jerome Biblical Commentary* (Englewood Cliffs, NJ: Prentice Hall, 1990)
PG	J. Migne (ed.), Patrologia graeca

PL	J. Migne (ed.), Patrologia latina
QD	Quaestiones disputatae
RAM	*Revue d'ascetique et mystique*
RivB	*Rivista biblica*
RSS	*Rome and the Study of Scripture* (rev. ed.; St, Meinrad, IN: Grail, 1962)
RSV	*Revised Standard Version* (of the Bible)
SBLRBS	Society of Biblical Literature Resources for Biblical Study
SBS	Stuttgarter Bibelstudien
SC	Sources chrétiennes
TGL	*Theologie und Glaube*
TQ	*Theologische Quartalschrift*
TS	*Theological Studies*
TToday	*Theology Today*
USQR	*Union Seminary Quarterly Review*
WUNT	Wissenschaftliche Untersuchungen zum Neuen Testament

PREFACE

The studies published here formed part of 1993 Anthony Jordan Lectures, delivered at Newman Theological College in Edmonton, Alberta in the Spring of this year. In recent years that annual lecture series has been devoted to various aspects of theology, and it was thought desirable that the series of 1993 be devoted to Scripture and its relation to Theology. I was invited to give these lectures, and I am grateful to the Oblates of Mary Immaculate of St. Mary's Province for this kind invitation, in particular to the Rev. Martin Moser, O.M.I., the Dean of the Theological College.

The overall theme of the 1993 Jordan Lectures is Scripture as the Soul of Theology. This title is derived immediately from the Second Vatican Council's Dogmatic Constitution on Divine Revelation (§24), which adopted the phrase from the encyclical of Pope Leo XIII, *Providentissimus Deus* (*ASS* 26 [1893–94] 283), the centenary of which we celebrated on 18 November of this year.

The first lecture, "Contemporary Approaches to Scripture," was devoted to the hermeneutical problem of how one should interpret Scripture today. The second, "Scripture, the Source of Theology," dealt more directly with the role that Scripture should play in the study of theology. And the third, "Scripture, the Bridge in Ecumenism," treated the way in which Scripture has been functioning in dialogues and bilateral consultations of Catholics with their Separated Brethren

1

in other Christian communities, and specifically in the
Catholic-Lutheran dialogue in the United States, in which I
had been a participant since 1973.

The first lecture was a considerably reworked form of an
article that I contributed earlier to the fiftieth-anniversary issue of *Theological Studies*, entitled, "Historical Criticism: Its
Role in Biblical Interpretation and Church Life" (50 [1989]
244–59). That first lecture has been further reworked and now
appears in this book in the first two chapters. The other two
lectures were freshly written for the occasion and are presented here in a slightly revised form in chapters 3 and 4.

What I have recorded in these four chapters is, in effect,
my recollection of and reaction to the way the Catholic Biblical Movement in North America developed since I first began
to teach Scripture in a Jesuit seminary, Woodstock College
in Maryland, in 1958. At that time, the movement was just
beginning, and in the course of three and a half decades it has
developed in ways that are familiar to all. The rebirth of interest in the Bible among Roman Catholics was occasioned by
another encyclical, *Divino afflante Spiritu*, which Pope Pius
XII issued in 1943 to commemorate the fiftieth anniversary
of Leo XIII's encyclical. Unfortunately, the new encyclical appeared in the midst of the Second World War, at a time when
the minds of most human beings in America, Europe, and
across the world were preoccupied with things other than the
Bible and its interpretation. As we also celebrated on 30 September 1993 the fiftieth anniversary of this far more important encyclical on biblical studies, we realized how it took almost a decade or more before it began to make its impact on
the Catholic world at large. But it did make an impact, and
consequently we are quite aware today of the importance of
the Bible and its place in modern Catholic life. This has, in
effect, been the result of these two papal encyclicals promoting
the study of the Bible in the Church. So it was fitting that the

Jordan Lectures be devoted in this double-anniversary year to Scripture as the Soul of Theology.

Since those lectures were given and the two anniversaries have passed, it is important to realize that another church-document on biblical interpretation has recently been issued. Because 1993 was the double anniversary of the encyclicals of Leo XIII and Pius XII, many people thought that Pope John Paul II might also issue an encyclical of his own on the topic. He was, however, apparently too preoccupied with *Veritatis Splendor* to give thought to a biblical encyclical. But the Pontifical Biblical Commission had been working for almost three years on an important text, *L'Interpretation de la Bible dans l'Eglise*. When the work of the Commission was completed, the text was submitted to Pope John Paul II. At the time of the Commission's annual meeting in April 1993, His Holiness summoned the College of Cardinals resident in Rome, the Diplomatic Corps, the professors of the Biblical Institute, and the members of the Commission to a solemn audience in the Sala Clementina on Friday, 23 April. In an allocution, the Pope commemorated the double anniversary of the encyclicals and commented on the Commission's document. The text of his remarks appeared in *Osservatore Romano* on Saturday, 24 April 1993. The Commission's document has since been published: *The Interpretation of the Bible in the Church* (Vatican City: Libreria Editrice Vaticana, 1993). The French form was the original, and it was subsequently translated into English, German, Italian, Portuguese, and Spanish. A summary of it can be found in my article, "The Interpretation of the Bible in the Church," *America* 169/17 (27 November 1993) 12–15.

My thanks are due to various persons who have helped me in the production of this book: to Martin Moser, O.M.I., who suggested the topics of the lectures; to Otto H. Hentz, S.J., who read the manuscript; to Lawrence Boadt, C.S.P., who considered the manuscript for publication; and to Donald F. Brophy and his staff at Paulist Press, who helped to get the manuscript into book form. To all of them I am deeply grateful.

Joseph A. Fitzmyer, S.J.
Professor Emeritus, Biblical Studies
The Catholic University of America
Washington, DC 20064
Resident at:
Jesuit Community, Georgetown University,
Washington, DC 20057.

1. THE CONTEMPORARY APPROACH TO SCRIPTURE

Scripture has seen a variety of interpretations ever since it first came into being. The reason for that variety is obvious, when one recalls that Scripture, as the inspired Word of God in human language,[1] has been preserved among God's people for close to three millennia. Written in different languages, Aramaic, Greek, and Hebrew, over a long period of time, almost a millennium in duration, the Word of God has thus been couched in human words of great variety. What was composed in human language had to be interpreted, because it had been subject to time-conditioned formulations and its original message had at times become less clear with the passing of the centuries. The Books of Moses, the *Tôrāh* or the Pentateuch, enshrine for us many regulations by which God's people were expected to live and conduct themselves, but also many records and accounts of God's acts on behalf of the people that came to be known as the Hebrews, or as Israel. Prophets, called by God, continued to proclaim his Word among that people and eventually saw that their proclamation was set in writing. Still other human authors, moved by God's Spirit, compiled accounts about the kings of Judah and Israel and

---

[1] See J. Levie, *The Bible, Word of God in Words of Men* (London: Chapman; New York: Kenedy, 1961); R. E. Brown, " 'And the Lord Said'? Biblical Reflections on Scripture as the Word of God," *TS* 42 (1981) 3–19; "Communicating the Divine and Human in Scripture," *Origins* 22/1 (14 May 1992) 1–9.

about great events in the history of Israel, recorded its prayers and its psalms, and gathered its wisdom into yet other forms of the written Word of God.

Because that written Word of God was not uniform in its style but has been preserved in various literary genres and forms, it called in time for interpretation. Within what we Christians usually call the Old Testament, one can find already examples of how God's people in a later stage of its development looked back on and interpreted older parts of its Sacred Scripture. Thus, events of the Exodus were reread in Deutero-Isaiah in terms of the return from the Babylonian Captivity. A psalm ascribed to David, commemorating deliverance from the hands of his enemies (2 Sam 22:2–51), eventually became part of Israel's prayer book as Psalm 18 and thereby took on new meaning. Prophetic utterances of Jeremiah (25:11–12; 29:10) were later interpreted in Dan 9:1–27.

This interpretation of God's Word found still greater scope in the Christian Scriptures. For part of the tradition that grew up out of the words and deeds of Jesus of Nazareth, which was eventually codified in the New Testament, became the written Word of God for his new people brought into being by the ministry, death, and resurrection of his Son. Yet this new form of the written Word depended heavily on God's Word of old. It not only built on it, but interpreted it anew in the light of the Christ-event.

Interpretation of the written Word of God has, then, been with us from before the dawn of Christianity. It took on an added form when the Hebrew Scriptures were translated at first into Greek, and then into Aramaic, Latin, Syriac, and other local languages, for each translation became an interpretation. The written Word of God has, consequently, been understood over the centuries in many ways, being invariably linked to the living culture, spirituality, and piety of God's people, which did not remain stagnant. Contemporary interpretation of Scripture is no different. As Christians of the twentieth century, we turn to the Bible to listen to the message that it continues to address to us today, precisely as people who live in a sophisticated western culture, shaped in recent centuries by the Renaissance, the Reformation, the Enlightenment, the age of science, industry, and technology. But we turn to it not as literalists, but as modern thinking Christians.

The mode of interpretation that has been dominant in the twentieth century is called the historical-critical method. It seeks to establish by techniques of historical and literary criticism the ancient foundations of the people of God and of the Christian Church and to understand the meaning of the ancient records of God's dealings with his people and of the ministry of Jesus of Nazareth and its sequel. It is the method advocated by the majority of centrist interpreters of the Bible, even though it often encounters criticism. For it has had its ups and downs; it has been used and abused. Calls are heard today to replace it with allegedly more adequate modes of interpretation: a post-critical approach to Scripture, a more literary interpretation, a rhetorical approach, a narrative approach, a structuralist approach, or a feminist approach. At times one even hears an appeal for a return to precritical interpretation, to the patristic or a spiritual interpretation.

What should one make of all these methods, approaches, and suggestions? What is valid or worthwhile among them? These are the questions I should like to address. In this first chapter I shall begin my discussion of contemporary modes of interpreting Scripture by treating the historical-critical method. That will be followed in chapter 2 by a consideration of other approaches to the understanding of Scripture.

What, then, is the historical-critical method? To answer that, I shall take up four aspects of the method: (I) its origin and development; (II) description of the method; (III) presuppositions with which the method is used; and (IV) problems that the method raises.

I. *Origin and Development*

The historical-critical method of biblical interpretation has been the dominant mode of interpretation in recent centuries, used by Catholic, Jewish, and Protestant interpreters of the Bible.[2]

Its roots are ancient, since it is ultimately derived from the Alexandrian School of interpretation in late Hellenistic times, especially under the Ptolemies who founded the library at Alexandria and attracted famous grammarians, rhetoricians, and philosophers to the Museion.[3] Though the method used then appears today somewhat primitive, it constituted a critical effort to ascertain the correct form of ancient texts, the philological meaning of the Homeric epics and other classical Greek literature, and the literal sense of the venerable books of Greeks and Barbarians. Eventually it was used of the literature even of Jews and Christians.[4] It was the mode of interpretation

---

[2] See E. Krentz, *The Historical-Critical Method* (Philadelphia, PA: Fortress, 1975); T. R. Curtin, *Historical Criticism and the Theological Interpretation of Scripture: The Catholic Discussion of a Biblical Hermeneutic: 1958–1983* (Rome: Dissertation, Gregorian University, Faculty of Theology, 1987). For a good account of the method as applied to the Old Testament, see H.-J. Kraus, *Geschichte der historisch-kritischen Erforschung des Alten Testaments* (3d ed.; Neukirchen: Neukirchener-V., 1982); and for the New Testament, see W. G. Kümmel, *The New Testament: The History of the Investigation of Its Problems* (Nashville, TN/New York: Abingdon, 1972). Cf. H. F. Hahn, *Old Testament in Modern Research* (Philadelphia, PA: Muhlenberg, 1954).

[3] See R. Pfeiffer, *History of Classical Scholarship from the Beginnings to the End of the Hellenistic Age* (Oxford: Clarendon, 1968) 87–279; H. I. Marrou, *A History of Education in Antiquity* (London: Sheed and Ward, 1956) 160–216, esp. 165–75.

[4] To this Alexandrian school we owe the translation of the Old Testament into Greek, which began under Ptolemy II Philadelphus. Related to it were the later inter-

employed at first by Origen, the great biblical interpreter, who brought to his task the grammatical, literary, and philosophical training of his time.[5] It was also utilized by Augustine and Jerome among the Church Fathers of the Western Church.[6]

Along with the quest of the literal meaning, an allegorical interpretation of Scripture was also developed, especially by Origen[7] and some of his followers. That allegorical interpretation met with no little opposition on the part of Lucian of Antioch, who objected to its excesses and brought into existence the Antiochene school of literal interpretation.[8] How-

---

pretations of the Bible by Philo, who sought to cast the teaching of the Jewish Scriptures into Greek philosophical categories and made elaborate use of Alexandrian allegory, which also emerged in this famous center of ancient culture and study.

[5] Origen made use of it in his attempt to establish the critical text of the Old Testament: *Hexapla* (see F. Field, *Origenis Hexaplorum quae supersunt* [2 vols.; Oxford: Clarendon, 1875]), especially in his work on the fifth column, the text of the Septuagint, which he sought to establish as best he could, in comparing it with the Hebrew (which he read only with great difficulty) and with the other Greek versions of Aquila, Symmachus, and Theodotion (where this existed).

[6] Augustine used a form of it in his opus, *De consensu evangelistarum libri quattuor* (CSEL 43 [1904]). See also his *De doctrina christiana libri quattuor*, where he expounds some of his theory of interpretation (1.1; 2.18; 3.86 [CSEL 80. 8, 38, 102]). Jerome's use can be found especially in his commentaries on the Prophets (e.g., *Commentariorum in Esaiam libri I-XI* [CCLat 73 (1963)]), in which he translated the Hebrew (= the Vulgate) along with Septuagint variants, and discussed others in Origen's *Hexapla*, together with a literal commentary, and often a spiritual exposition of the passage relating it to Christ or the Church. See J. N. D. Kelly, *Jerome: His Life, Writings and Controversies* (London: Duckworth, 1975) passim; R. F. Collins, "Augustine of Hippo Precursor of Modern Biblical Scholarship," *Louvain Studies* 12 (1987) 131–51; H. Merkel, *Die Widersprüche zwischen den Evangelien: Ihre polemische und apologetische Behandlung in der Alten Kirche bis zu Augustin* (WUNT 13; Tübingen: Mohr [Siebeck], 1971).

[7] J. Quasten says of it: "It is not true that this method was for him only a means of eliminating the Old Testament, for which, on the contrary, he had the highest regard. But it is true that he thus introduced into exegesis a dangerous subjectivism leading to arbitrariness and error" (*Patrology* [3 vols.; Westminster, MD: Newman, 1950–60] 2. 42).

[8] Ibid., 2. 142–43.

ever, the two modes, the literal and the allegorical, character-
ized most of the interpretation of the Bible in the patristic and
medieval eras.

More immediately the roots of the historical-critical
method of biblical interpretation are traced to the Renaissance, especially to its emphasis on *recursus ad fontes*, "get-
ting back to the sources," which involved the study of classical
Greek, the Semitic languages, and the writings of ancient authors whose works had long been neglected in the antecedent
Dark Ages.[9] Then the quest of the literal sense of Scripture
was undertaken in a renewed way with all the techniques developed at this time. The almost contemporary Copernican
revolution also had a important bearing on the study of the
literal sense of the Bible, especially in its aftermath, the Gali-
leo Affair, which was involved in the interpretation of Josh 10:
12–13 about the sun standing still. To this period is traced the
study of the Bible in its original languages, Aramaic, Greek,
and Hebrew, instead of the Latin Vulgate, which had been
practically the only Bible in use in the intervening periods in
the Western Church since Jerome.

Although the Reformers, Martin Luther and Jean Cal-
vin, did not radically depart from traditional interpretation of
Scripture, they gave Scripture a primacy over the Church and
its interpretation of the Bible that resulted in an abandonment
of much of the allegorical interpretation and in an emphasis
on the literal sense of Scripture, especially as it was read in the
original languages and from which it was then being translated
widely into the vernacular.

In the seventeenth and eighteenth centuries the
historical-critical method was further developed through the

---

[9] See W. Neil, "The Criticism and Theological Use of the Bible," *The Cambridge History of the Bible* (3 vols.; Cambridge, UK: Cambridge University, 1970,
1969, 1963) 3. 238–93.

work of the Dutch jurist and theologian Hugo Grotius, the French Oratorian and biblical scholar Richard Simon, and the Dutch philosopher Baruch Spinoza—thus through the work of a Protestant, a Catholic, and a Jew.

Further impetus was given to this method of biblical interpretation at the time of the Enlightenment and by the movement of German historicism in the nineteenth century. There were, on the one hand, the deist attacks on traditional Christianity. The eighteenth-century deist Hermann Samuel Reimarus had already penned such an attack in *Apologie, oder Schützschrift für die vernünftigen Verehrer Gottes* (completed in 1767), but fear of consequences that might ensue deterred him from publishing it during his lifetime. After his death (1768), seven parts of an early draft of his work were published by the philosopher Gotthold Ephraim Lessing under the title *Fragmente des Wolfenbüttelschen Ungenannten* (1774–78).[10] Reimarus' work led eventually to the so-called Life of Jesus research (*Leben-Jesu Forschung*) of the mid-nineteenth century. On the other hand, there was the influence of Leopold von Ranke, who as a historian made it his ambition to present the past *wie es eigentlich gewesen*, "as it really was."[11] That ambitious goal of "objective historiography" affected many biblical interpreters of the time, who

---

[10] See *Fragmente des Wolfenbüttelschen Ungenannten. Ein Anhang zu dem Fragment vom Zweck Jesu und seiner Jünger* (Berlin, 1788; 5th ed.; Berlin: Reimer, 1895); *Von dem Zweck Jesu und seiner Jünger: Noch ein Fragment des Wolfenbüttelschen Ungenannten* (Berlin: Wever, 1784). Reimarus's son disclosed the identity of the unnamed author only in 1814. The complete manuscript of Reimarus is said to have been published only in 1972, *Apologie: Oder Schützschrift für die vernünftigen Verehrer Gottes* (2 vols.; Frankfurt: Insel Verlag). Cf. *Reimarus Fragments* (ed. C. H. Talbert; Lives of Jesus Series; Philadelphia, PA: Fortress, 1970); H. S. Reimarus, *The Goal of Jesus and His Disciples* (ed. G. W. Buchanan; Leiden: Brill, 1970).

[11] *Geschichte der romanischen und germanischen Völker von 1494 bis 1514: Zur Kritik neuerer Geschichtschreiber* (Sämmtliche Werke 33–34; 3d ed.; Leipzig: Duncker & Humblot, 1885) vii ("er will bloss zeigen, wie es eigentlich gewesen").

strove to write the history of Israel or to depict anew the beginnings of Christianity. Then scholars such as Ferdinand
Christian Baur, Heinrich E. G. Paulus, David Friedrich
Strauss, Bruno Bauer, and Ernest Renan composed their studies of the historical Jesus, while treating the Gospels merely as
ancient human records.

Likewise contributing to the development of the
historical-critical method of interpreting Scripture were the
great historical and archaeological discoveries of the late eighteenth and nineteenth centuries. Events and facts of ancient
history came to light in a way that was unknown in previous
centuries, even at the time of the Renaissance and Reformation. These discoveries impinged on biblical history, on the
history of ancient Israel, and on the beginnings of early Christianity in a way that was previously unsuspected.

The Rosetta Stone, written in hieroglyphic Egyptian, De-
motic, and Greek, was discovered by an officer in Napoleon's
Egyptian Expeditionary Force in the western delta of the Nile
in 1798–99. But it was not until 1827 that Jean François
Champollion succeeded in deciphering its hieroglyphic writing.[12] It took about a half century more before that key un-
locked the treasures of Egyptian literature. Then for the first
time the Old Testament was read against the literary background of Israel's neighbor to the west. Israel's poetry, wisdom
literature, and even some of its historical writings were then
compared for the first time with their Egyptian counterparts.

Similarly, the literature of ancient Assyria and Babylonia
became known to Old Testament scholars through the decipherment of the ancient Bisitun inscription of the Persian
king Darius the Great, which is still *in situ* along the old cara-

---

[12] See J. Finegan, *Light from the Ancient Past: The Archaeological Background of Judaism and Christianity* (2 vols.; Princeton: Princeton University, 1974) 1. 90, 133–34.

van road from Babylon to Ecbatana (modern Hamadan, in northwestern Iran). Written in Old Persian, Elamite, and Akkadian, it had stood there for centuries until an Englishman, Henry C. Rawlinson, made copies of it in 1835. Its Akkadian cuneiform version was finally deciphered in 1846, in which the German scholar G. F. Grotefend was also largely involved.[13] Eventually the Old Testament could be read and studied against the background of the literature of ancient Assyria and Babylonia, Israel's neighbors to the east. The unexpected recovery of this ancient historical, legal, poetical, astronomical, and epistolary literature made it clear that the Old Testament, the biblical heritage of ancient Israel, could no longer be interpreted in isolation, for it was part of the cultural heritage of the ancient Near East, related to the literary culture of Egypt, Assyria, and Babylonia.

Moreover, the nineteenth-century discovery of thousands of Greek papyri in Egypt brought to light forms of Greek literature, legal documents, and letters that radically affected the study of the Septuagint and the New Testament. In the course of the twentieth century other historical and archaeological discoveries, especially in Syria and Palestine, shed further light on the biblical texts.[14] Valuable historical and literary material was recovered in 1929 at Ras Shamra in Syria,

---

[13] Rawlinson first deciphered the Old Persian text, and that led to the decipherment of the two other languages. See further J. Finegan, *Light* (n. 12 above), 234–36. In the early part of the twentieth century an Aramaic version of the inscription was discovered among papyri from Elephantine in Egypt. See J. C. Greenfield and B. Porten, *The Bisitun Inscription of Darius the Great: Aramaic Version* (Corpus inscriptionum iranicarum 1/5; London: Lund Humphries, 1982).

[14] Discoveries of ancient documents continued and continue to be made in Egypt and in the area of ancient Mesopotamia, but they have not been as significant or as dramatic as the earlier discoveries in these areas. The sole exception might be the recovery of many ancient Aramaic documents from numerous places in Egypt such as Elephantine, Saqqara, etc., which came to light only in the twentieth century. See J. A. Fitzmyer and S. A. Kaufman, *An Aramaic Bibliography, Part I: Old, Official,*

where cuneiform, alphabetic texts brought to light a new Northwest-Semitic language, which preserved Ugaritic literature with many important Canaanite parallels to Hebrew poetry.[15] Again, the discovery of scrolls in eleven caves of the Qumran area (1947–1956) have contributed much to the critical study of the Old Testament text and to the historical study of the Palestinian Jewish culture in which Christianity and its New Testament find their matrix.[16]

These discoveries of the eighteenth, nineteenth, and twentieth centuries brought to light facts of ancient history and examples of ancient literature that were unknown to the interpreters of the patristic, medieval, and renaissance periods. The Fathers of the Church, the scholastic theologians, and even the scholars of the Renaissance knew nothing of these neighboring cultures and were unable to interpret the Bible in the light of them. Such historical facts and ancient literatures a modern reader of the Bible cannot ignore, for they have radically affected our understanding of the written Word of God and of how it has to be interpreted today.

Along with many others, the Catholic Church reacted to these modern discoveries that affected the interpretation of the Bible and to the modes of interpretation that made use of them. At the beginning of this century, Pope Leo XIII set up the Pontifical Biblical Commission (1902).[17] Ostensibly it was

---

and Biblical Aramaic (Baltimore, MD/London: The Johns Hopkins University, 1992).

[15] Hundreds of clay tablets were discovered by chance; they were deciphered almost immediately by H. Bauer of Germany and E. Dhorme and C. Virolleaud of France. See further J. Finegan, *Light* (n. 12 above), 171–74.

[16] See G. Vermes, *The Dead Sea Scrolls: Qumran in Perspective* (rev. ed.; Philadelphia, PA: Fortress, 1981); *The Dead Sea Scrolls in English* (3d ed.; London: Penguin Group, 1987); J. A. Fitzmyer, *The Dead Sea Scrolls: Major Publications and Tools for Study* (SBLRBS 20; Atlanta, GA: Scholars, 1990); *Responses to 101 Questions on the Dead Sea Scrolls* (New York/Mahwah, NJ: Paulist, 1992).

[17] *ASS* 25 (1902–3) 234–38; *EB* §538–69; *RSS* §137–48.

to promote biblical studies in the Church in light of these new discoveries and developments, but it was also to guard against excessive critical interpretations of the Bible. The latter were seen to stem from the rationalist spirit with which much of the critical interpretation of the Bible in the nineteenth century had been conducted in the wake of the Enlightenment. The first word of Leo's apostolic letter, *Vigilantiae,* set the tone for the activity of the Commission in the first third of the twentieth century. Many of the Commission's eventual *responsa,* often wrongly called "decrees," were negative reactions to proposals made by biblical interpreters using the historical-critical method: responses about the Mosaic authorship of the Pentateuch, the Synoptic Problem, and the historical character of the canonical Gospels.[18] The Commission never condemned the method itself, but the effect of its responses was to cast a dark cloud of reaction and fear over Catholic biblical scholarship in the early part of the twentieth century.[19] It de-

---

[18] The *responsa* are conveniently found in *EB* §160–61, 181–84, 187–89, 276–80, 324–40, 383-416, 496, 513–14; in English in *RSS,* 117–38 (with the same marginal numbers as in *EB*). For a convenient summary of them and their background, see *NJBC* art. 72 (pp. 1166–74).

[19] Apropos of the situation at that time in the United States, G. P. Fogarty writes:

> The state of Catholic biblical scholarship in the United States at the end of the 1920s was bleak. Whatever scholarship there had been at the beginning of the century had either been destroyed in the wake of Modernism or had gone underground. . . . The type of neo-Thomism, formulated in the nineteenth century to combat rationalism, had become so pervasive that Catholic writers confused theology with doctrine. . . . Professors . . . took as their starting point, not the criticism of texts, but the declarations of the popes or the Biblical Commission. . . . In effect, integrism had become a habit of mind, even after Benedict XV had condemned it. The American church gave little indication that it was ready to undertake any type of scholarly endeavor (*American Catholic Biblical*

terred most Catholic interpreters from using the historical-
critical method.

It remained for the great Dominican founder of the Ecole
Biblique of Jerusalem, M.-J. Lagrange, to show that the
historical-critical method could be used rightly by orthodox
interpreters of the Bible. His small book, *La méthode historique*, first published in 1903, clearly argued that the method
was in itself neutral.[20] Though Lagrange suffered much from
the integrists of his day, his contribution to the debate and the
many commentaries that he wrote on Old and New Testament books, utilizing the historical-critical method, are recalled with gratitude today.

The cloud of negative reaction to this method of biblical
interpretation was finally lifted when Pope Pius XII issued his
encyclical *Divino afflante Spiritu* in 1943,[21] in which, though
he did not mention the method as such, he made it clear that
Catholic interpreters were henceforth to use its principles. He
insisted on (1) the study of the Bible in its original languages;
(2) the proper use of textual criticism; (3) the interpretation of
the Bible according to its ancient texts, and not merely the
Latin Vulgate, which was to be understood to enjoy a juridi-
cal, not a critical, authenticity; (4) the interpretation of the
Bible according to its literal sense; (5) the role of patristic in-

---

Scholarship: *A History from the Early Republic to Vatican II* [San Francisco, CA: Harper & Row, 1989] 198).

[20] First published as *La méthode historique surtout à propos de l'Ancien Testament* (Paris: Lecoffre, 1903), it soon appeared in an *édition augmentée* (Paris: Lecoffre, 1904). Cf. *Historical Criticism and the Old Testament* (London: Catholic
Truth Society, 1905), a translation of the 1904 edition. Also F.-M. Braun, *The Work
of Père Lagrange* (Milwaukee: Bruce, 1963) 66–100; *Père Lagrange: Personal Reflections and Memories* (New York: Paulist, 1985) 106–14.

[21] *AAS* 35 (1943) 297–325; *EB* §538–69; *RSS* §538–69. Cf. J. R. Donahue, "A
Journey Remembered: Catholic Biblical Scholarship 50 Years after *Divino Afflante
Spiritu*," *America* 169/7 (18 September 1993) 6–11.

terpretation in the Church; (6) the character of the sacred human writer; (7) the proper regard for the ancient literary forms that the inspired human author had employed; and (8) the application to the biblical text of modern discoveries: "either in the domain of archaeology or ancient history or literature, as well as their manner and art of reasoning, narrating, and writing" (§40).[22] That insistence of Pius XII eventually freed Catholic biblical interpretation from its own form of literalism, which had been inherited from the post-Tridentine era.

Significantly, and indeed in light of immediate antecedents of the encyclical,[23] Pius XII realized the need to spell out the importance of the literal meaning of the sacred text:

In the performance of this task let the interpreters bear in mind that their foremost and greatest endeavor should be to discern and define clearly that sense of the biblical words which is called literal. Aided by the context and comparison with similar passages, let them therefore by means of their knowledge of languages search out with all diligence the literal meaning of the words; all these helps indeed are wont to be pressed into service in the explana-

---

[22] See further H. Cazelles, "Anwendung und Erfahrungen mit der historisch-kritischen Methode in der katholischen Exegese," *Die historisch-kritische Methode und die heutige Suche nach einem lebendigen Verständnis der Bibel* (ed. H. Riedlinger; Freiburg im B.: Katholische Akademie; Munich: Schnell & Steiner, 1985) 72–88.

[23] An anonymous brochure, entitled *A Most Grave Danger for the Church, and for Souls: The Critical-scientific System of Studying and Interpreting Holy Scripture, Its Evil Misconceptions and Aberrations,* had been sent to Bishops and Superiors of Religious Congregations in Italy. It condemned the historical-critical method and advocated instead a type of exegesis called "meditative." It was subsequently learned that the author was Dolindo Ruotolo, a priest who wrote under the pen name of Dain Cohenel. Because of it the Biblical Commission addressed a letter to all the Bishops and Religious Superiors of Italy on 20 August 1941 (see *EB* §522–33; *RSS* §522–33). This was part of the immediate background of Pius XII's encyclical.

tion also of profane writers, so that the mind of the author may be made abundantly clear (§23).

The recommendation of the historical-critical method was thus ordered to ascertaining the literal sense of Scripture. This recommendation, however, did not die with Pius XII. In 1964 the Biblical Commission issued an instruction *On the Historical Truth of the Gospels,*[24] which did not merely reaffirm the historicity of the canonical Gospels but proved to be a nuanced, enlightened discussion of the three stages of the gospel tradition. It thus emerged that the most important word in the title of the instruction was not the adjective "historical," as might have been expected, but the preposition "on." For the Commission insisted:

> Unless the exegete pays attention to all these things [the three stages of the gospel tradition] which pertain to the origin and composition of the Gospels and makes proper use of all the laudable achievements of recent research, he will not fulfill his task of probing into what the sacred writers intended and what they really said (par. X).

Among the "laudable achievements" the Commission itself singled out the "reasonable elements" of the form-critical method, which it mentioned explicitly by name (par. V). Thus a refinement of the method itself that had been derived from non-Catholic interpreters of the Bible received clear approbation, but the Commission took pains to distinguish it from

---

[24] *Sancta Mater Ecclesia,* in *AAS* 56 (1964) 712–18; cf. DS §3999–99e. A translation of this instruction, along with a commentary on it, can be found in the appendix of my book, *A Christological Catechism: New Testament Answers: New Revised and Expanded Edition* (New York/Mahwah, NJ: Paulist, 1991) 119–62. The Latin text and an English translation are also published in *CBQ* 26 (1964) 299–312.

the presuppositions with which it had sometimes been used. Moreover, the substance of that instruction was taken up by the Fathers at the Second Vatican Council and became part of the dogmatic constitution on Divine Revelation (§19).[25]

II. *Description*

This method of biblical interpretation is called "historical-critical" because it borrows its techniques from both historical and literary criticism. It recognizes that the Bible, though it is the inspired written Word of God, is an ancient record, composed by many human authors over a long period of time. As such, it has to be read, studied, and analyzed as other ancient records of human history. Since the Bible narrates events that affected the lives of ancient Jews and early Christians, its various accounts have to be read, compared, and analyzed in their original languages, against their proper human and historical backgrounds, and within their contemporary contexts. In effect, this method applies to the Bible all the critical techniques of classical philology, and in doing so, it refuses a priori to exclude any critical analysis in its quest for the meaning of the sacred and inspired text. It is called a "critical" method, not because it criticizes the Bible or seeks to evoke skepticism about the historical record of the ancient

---

[25] *Dei Verbum* §19; *AAS* 58 (1966) 826–27; cf. W. M. Abbott, *The Documents of Vatican II* (New York: Herder and Herder and Association Press, 1966) 124. An English translation of this paragraph can likewise be found in the appendix of *A Christological Catechism* (n. 24 above), 163–64.

See further H. Vorgrimler (ed.), *Commentary on the Documents of Vatican II* (5 vols.; London: Burns and Oates, 1967–69) 3.252–61; O. Semmelroth and M. Zerwick, *Vaticanum II über das Wort Gottes: Die Konstitution "Dei Verbum": Einführung und Kommentar, Text und Übersetzung* (SBS 16; Stuttgart: Katholisches Bibelwerk, 1966) 44–50.

text, but because it compares and analyzes its details in an effort to arrive at a historical and literary judgment about it.

The method utilizes two preliminary steps, borrowed from classical philology: (1) *introductory questions* and (2) *textual criticism*. The first step raises the introductory questions and deals with: (a) the authenticity of the writing (e.g., Did David compose the psalm? Did Paul write the Epistle to the Ephesians?); (b) the integrity or unity of the writing (e.g., Is chapter 16 an original part of the Pauline letter to the Romans?); (c) the date and place of composition; (d) the content of the writing, analyzed according to its structure, outline, style, and literary form (Is it a letter, a narrative, an apocalypse, a sermon?); (e) the occasion and purpose of the writing (i.e., the author's intention in composing it, as this is evident in the writing); and (f) its literary background (Has the author been influenced by Assyrian, Egyptian, Canaanite, Palestinian Jewish, or Hellenistic ideas?). All such preliminary questions help much in the understanding of the biblical writing that comes to us from a definite literary context, time, and place in antiquity.

The second step, textual criticism, is likewise borrowed from classical philology. It deals with the transmission of the biblical text in its original language and in ancient versions: In what manuscripts is the best form of the text preserved? What is the best family of manuscripts? Does an ancient version reflect a better reading, one possibly superior to the transmitted Hebrew, Aramaic, or Greek text? This complicated, technical aspect of biblical interpretation is clearly important and fundamental.

But the historical-critical method of interpreting the Bible does not stop with such preliminary considerations, even though they seriously affect the critical judgment of any text. Along with such preliminary questions are the techniques of historical criticism itself that enable one to judge how much of biblical text truly reflects ancient reality. Since Hellenistic times this has meant the critical assessment of the testimony of ancient writers who pass on records of past events or past utterances. For instance, since the "Our Father" is transmitted to Christian believers in two different forms (Matt 6:9–13 and Luke 11:2–4), historical criticism would seek to determine which form is more likely the words used by Jesus himself.[26]

But in addition to such critical assessment there are refinements of the method that have come to be associated with it over the centuries and decades. Such are:

(1) *Literary criticism*, which analyzes the literary and stylistic character of the biblical text. This is related to one of the preliminary questions already mentioned (see d above), but it is pursued also as part of the method itself and has long been associated with historical criticism. It is important, because it can curb the historical judgment about a given text. When one sees that an ancient writer has written poetry of a definite kind or has employed rhetorical devices (modes of persuasive argumentation, *inclusio, chiasmus*, catchword bonding), or has argued from cause to effect, or from effect to cause, one may realize that the historical aspect of the writing may not have been the principal or primary concern of its author.

(2) *Source criticism* is another refinement of the historical-critical method of biblical interpretation. It seeks to determine the prehistory of a biblical book. What sources did the biblical writer use in composing the book? In some cases the biblical text simply cries out for source analysis because of its parallel accounts or doublet narratives of the same event, its stereotyped phraseology, etc. If the book is part of the Penta-

---

[26] See my commentary, *The Gospel according to Luke* (AB 28, 28A; Garden City, NY: Doubleday, 1981, 1985) 896–901.

teuch, the interpreter has to analyze the differences of composition among the Yahwist, Elohist, Deuteronomist, and Priestly writings. If the text is part of a Synoptic Gospel, the recognition of it as derived from Mark, or "Q," or from a private Matthean or Lucan source is an important factor in the interpretation of the passage. Source criticism, however, is not an end in itself, and the interpreter's task is far from finished, once the source of a passage has been determined. Yet the difference in the parallels or doublets, analyzed as derived from difference sources, often affects the historical judgment about a text and usually aids in the final understanding of its literary and religious message.

(3) *Form criticism* is a third refinement. It was applied first to the Old Testament by H. Gunkel as *Gattungsgeschichte*.[27] It was further developed in the interpretation of the Synoptic Gospels by K. L. Schmidt, M. Dibelius, and R. Bultmann at the beginning of the twentieth century. It seeks to specify the literary form or subform of a given biblical passage. What kind of a psalm is it? Is the text apocalyptic or sapiential? Is the gospel episode a parable or other type of saying of Jesus, a miracle story, or a pronouncement story?[28] Such forms are diverse, and one learns from form criticism to shift mental gears in reading biblical passages. One does not read or interpret the beatitudes the same way one interprets a miracle story. One also learns much about how the form has developed within a given tradition or different traditions, and for this reason it is called in German *Formgeschichte*, the history of the form. The form-

---

[27] See J. Muilenburg, "Form Criticism and Beyond," *JBL* 88 (1969) 1–18; repr. in *The Bible in Its Literary Milieu* (ed. J. Maier and V. Tollers; Grand Rapids, MI: Eerdmans, 1979) 362–80.

[28] See V. Taylor, *The Formation of the Gospel Tradition* (London: Macmillan, 1949).

critical analysis of biblical passages affects one's historical judgment about them and reveals how the truth of a passage is analogous to its form.[29] Herein lies the crucial relationship of form criticism to historical criticism.

(4) *Redaction criticism* is yet another refinement of the historical-critical method, because it seeks to determine how certain biblical writers, using traditional materials, have shaped, modified, edited, or redacted the source material they have inherited from writers or from community traditions before them in the interest of their own literary and religious goal or purpose. Such redaction is often evident in the language and style of a given biblical writer. Once such redaction is discerned, it too has a bearing on the historical judgment of a passage.

All such critical techniques, historical and literary, are geared to one end: to determine the meaning of the sacred text as it was intended by the human author moved long ago to compose it and to ascertain what it is saying to us today. Since the truth that has been enshrined in the author's text is analogous to the form used, such historical criticism teaches us that we cannot read an ancient text without the sophisticated understanding that the form itself calls for. Thus, for instance, we have learned from this method that not everything that is narrated in the past tense necessarily corresponds to ancient reality, and that not everything put on the lips of Jesus of Nazareth by evangelists was necessarily uttered by him, even though the four evangelists have passed on to us "the honest truth about Jesus."[30]

---

[29] As A. Bea once put it, "Sua cuique generi literario est veritas" (Each literary form has its own truth). See *De sacrae Scripturae inspiratione* (2d ed.; Rome: Biblical Institue, 1935) 106 §90.

[30] As *Dei verbum* phrased it: "ita semper ut vera et sincera de Iesu nobis communicarent" (§19). One should consult the Acta of Vatican Council II for the details

Similarly, from such criticism we have learned in regard to the Gospels to distinguish three stages of the gospel tradition: (I) what Jesus of Nazareth did and said (corresponding roughly to A.D. 1–33); (II) what disciples preached about him, about his words and about his deeds (corresponding roughly to A.D. 33–65); and (III) what evangelists wrote about him, having culled, synthesized, and explicated the tradition that preceded them, each in his own way and in a manner suited to his own literary and religious purpose (corresponding roughly to A.D. 65–95). The relationship of Stage III to Stages I and II is *the* problem for twentieth-century readers of the Gospels, and herein lies the crucial need of the historical-critical method of gospel interpretation. To disregard it and to equate Stage III with Stage I is the path of Fundamentalism.

What is all-important in this regard is that, if one can determine by the historical-critical method that Jesus of Nazareth did not utter some of the words attributed to him in the Gospels (e.g., all the phrases of the Matthean form of the "Our Father"), that does not mean that the Matthean additions are unimportant or have no relevance for the spiritual life of Christian readers of the New Testament today. In this regard, even the believing practitioners of the historical-critical method admit that such Matthean additions would be inspired and that they have been inherited from the early Church's tradition about Jesus, which is a Spirit-guaranteed heritage destined by God as a means of building up the spiritual lives of Christians. The inspired Matthean form of the "Our Father" passes on to Christians of all generations a true understanding of Jesus, one expressive of what his word to all of us really is, one expressive of our relation to God the Father.

---

of the debate that ensued apropos of the composition of this clause; see H. Vorgrimler (ed.), *Commentary* (n. 25 above), 3.256–59.

III. *Presuppositions*

One reason why the historical-critical method sometimes falls under suspicion today is that it was tainted at important stages of its development by presuppositions that are not necessarily part of it.

It was tainted by the rationalist presuppositions with which the *Leben-Jesu Forschung* once used it. The *Fragmente* of Reimarus and the lives of Jesus by Baur, Strauss, Renan, and others stemmed either from deist attacks on historical Christianity or from historical studies that sought to liberate from dogmatic influence the Gospels, which were to be analyzed solely as records of antiquity. Adolf von Harnack, the patrologist and church historian, sought to curb the extreme tendencies of this allegedly presuppositionless study of the historical Jesus and emphasized a respect for tradition. But he never abandoned the historical-critical method itself.[31] It remained for Albert Schweitzer to unmask the effort of the Life of Jesus research. In his famous book *The Quest of the Historical Jesus*, Schweitzer showed that such investigation of Jesus' life had sprung not from a purely historical interest in him, but from a "struggle against the tyranny of dogma," and that the greatest of such "lives" of Jesus, those by Reimarus and Strauss, had been "written with hate"—"not so much hate of the Person of Jesus as of the supernatural nimbus with which it was so easy to surround him."[32] Thus rationalist attacks on traditional Christianity, especially its supernatural aspects,

---

[31] Von Harnack realized that, if "historical knowledge and critical reflection" were disdained, the gospel would be in danger of being "given over into the hands of devotional preachers who freely create their own understanding of the Bible and who set up their own dominion" (*Christliche Welt* [Leipzig: Hinrichs, 1923] 50–51).

[32] *The Quest of the Historical Jesus: A Critical Study of Its Progress from Reimarus to Wrede* (London: Black, 1919; repr. 1948) 4–5.

were linked to an otherwise neutral method, which they tainted unduly. For what was at fault was the rationalist presupposition with which the method was used, not the method itself.

At a still later period the method was again used by Schmidt, Dibelius, and Bultmann in their form-critical study of the Synoptics. Bultmann's contribution proved to be the most influential,[33] as he linked historical criticism with a form of kerygmatic theology, which depended heavily on Luther's justification by faith alone, Strauss's mythical interpretation of the Gospels, and the early existentialist philosophy of M. Heidegger. Emphasis on the preached Word and justification *fide sola* resulted in Bultmann's lack of interest in Jesus of Nazareth himself, or in what he did or said in Nazareth, Capernaum, or Jerusalem. Bultmann was uninterested in any continuity between Stage I and the later stages of the gospel tradition and emphasized only what the gospel proclaims and how its preached Word accosts the individual believer of today. He thus sought to subordinate event to word; indeed, for him the word may be said to have generated the event. Hence Bultmann's favored treatment of the form called by him "apophthegm,"[34] the narrative in the gospel tradition that was preserved because of the pronouncement that it enshrined. The narrated event was unimportant so long as the reader of today was accosted by the pronouncement or punch line in

---

[33] "New Testament and Mythology," *Kerygma and Myth: A Theological Debate* (ed. H. W. Bartsch; London: SPCK, 1953) 1–44; *Theology of the New Testament* (2 vols.; London: SCM, 1952, 1955). Cf. D. E. Nineham, "Demythologization," *A Dictionary of Biblical Interpretation* (ed. R. J. Coggins and J. L. Houlden; London: SCM; Philadelphia, PA: Trinity Press International, 1990) 171–74.

[34] *History of the Synoptic Tradition* (Oxford; Blackwell, 1968) 11–69. M. Dibelius (*From Tradition to Gospel* [New York: Scribner, 1935]) called it a "paradigm," whereas V. Taylor (*Formation* [n. 28 above], 22–24, 29–30) more accurately labeled it a "pronouncement story."

it. Thus Bultmann was led to the demythologization of the event, and for him the quest for the historical basis of the kerygma was a betrayal of the principle of faith alone. Rather, New Testament theology begins with the primitive kerygma—and not before it.[35] The kerygma addresses us through the New Testament, and its Word is the basis as well as the object of our faith. Moreover, that preached Word has to be understood in a Heideggerian existentialist fashion, as it elicits from us a "yes," the affirmation of one's personal authentic existence. In reality, this authentic existence is a gift of God that comes from the opening of one's self to the grace of forgiveness announced in the kerygma.[36]

Yet, despite the laudable pastoral thrust of Bultmann's concern to make the New Testament message a challenge for people in the twentieth century, he associated the historical-critical method with philosophical and theological presuppositions that proved to be not universally acceptable.[37]

---

[35] *Theology* (n. 33 above), 3. See also p. 35: ". . . the personality of Jesus has no importance for the kerygma either of Paul or of John or for the New Testament in general. Indeed the tradition of the earliest Church did not even unconsciously preserve a picture of his personality. Every attempt to reconstruct one remains a play of subjective imagination." Cf. Bultmann's *Jesus and the Word* (New York: Scribner, 1958); *Jesus Christ and Mythology* (New York: Scribner, 1958); *Das Urchristentum im Rahmen der antiken Religionen* (Erasmus-Bibliothek; Zurich: Artemis, 1949; 2d ed., 1954).

[36] See futher J. Macquarrie, *An Existentialist Theology: A Comparison of Heidegger and Bultmann* (New York: Macmillan, 1955). Cf. B. Jaspert, *Rudolf Bultmanns Werk und Wirkung* (Darmstadt: Wissenschaftliche Buchgesellschaft, 1984); C. W. Kegley, *The Theology of Rudolf Bultmann* (London: SCM, 1966); N. Perrin, *The Promise of Bultmann* (Philadelphia, PA: Fortress, 1969).

[37] Bultmann's interpretation of the New Testament did not, however, go without its critics. See V. Taylor, *The Formation of the Gospel Tradition* (n. 28 above), 14: "Dibelius is liberal rather than radical; Bultmann is radical to the point of scepticism, and it is not strange that he has been looked upon as *Strauss redivivus*. If Bultmann is right, we have not only lost the Synoptic framework but also much the greater part of the material. The narratives are mainly legends and ideal constructions, and most of the sayings, while Palestinian in origin, are products of primitive Christianity which

The foregoing are but two examples of presuppositions with which the historical-critical method has been used: the rationalist, antidogmatic presupposition and the demythologizing, existentialist presupposition. Modern Christian practitioners of the method, however, also use the method with presuppositions—but with presuppositions of a quite different sort.

---

puts back its own ideas and beliefs into the lips of Jesus." Cf. E. Fascher, *Die formgeschichtliche Methode* (BZNW 2; Giessen: Töpelmann, 1924) 82–144; Evangelical Theological Faculty of the University of Tübingen, *Für und wider die Theologie Bultmanns* (Sammlung gemeinverständlicher Vorträge und Schriften aus dem Gebiet der Theologie und Religionsgeschichte 198–99; Tübingen: Mohr [Siebeck], 1952).

From a different perspective one should recall the reaction of the littérateur C. S. Lewis to Bultmann and to his claim that the personality of Jesus had no importance for the early kerygma (see n. 35 above). Lewis protests: "I am a sheep, telling shepherds what only a sheep can tell them. . . . Such are the reactions of one bleating layman to Modern Theology" ("Modern Theology and Biblical Criticism," *Christian Reflections* [ed. W. Hooper; London: G. Bles, 1967] 152–66). About Bultmann he wrote: "So there is no personality of Our Lord presented in the New Testament. Through what strange process has this learned German gone in order to make himself blind to what all men except him see? What evidence have we that he would recognize a personality if it were there? For it is Bultmann *contra mundum.* If anything whatever is common to all believers, and even to many unbelievers, it is the sense that in the Gospels they have met a personality. There are characters whom we know to be historical but of whom we do not feel that we have any personal knowledge—knowledge by acquaintance; such are Alexander, Attila, or William of Orange. There are others who make no claim to historical reality but whom, none the less, we know as we know real people: Falstaff, Uncle Toby, Mr Pickwick. But there are only three characters who, claiming the first sort of reality, also actually have the second. And surely everyone knows who they are: Plato's Socrates, the Jesus of the Gospels, and Boswell's Johnson . . ." (p. 156). See further L. Malevez, *The Christian Message and Myth: The Theology of Rudolf Bultmann* (London: SCM, 1958).

More recently Cardinal J. Ratzinger has added his criticism: "Biblical Interpretation in Crisis: On the Question of the Foundations and Approaches of Exegesis Today," *Biblical Interpretation in Crisis: The Ratzinger Conference on Bible and Church* (ed. R. J. Neuhaus; Grand Rapids, MI: Eerdmans and the Rockford Institute Center on Religion & Society, 1989) 1–23, esp. 8–16. See also the report of the discussion on pp. 109–12. Card. Ratzinger's paper appeared earlier (under a slightly different title) in *Origins* 17/35 (1988) 593–602; also in *This World* 22 (1988) 3–19.

To explain the presuppositions used by Catholic interpreters today, I have to say a word first about "exegesis," the term by which the interpretation of Scripture according to this method is often known. Greek *exēgēsis* is derived from the verb *exēgeisthai,* "draw out"; its aim is to draw out from a book or text the meaning of its words and phrases, and to explain its text as a whole.[38] Webster's *Third New International Dictionary* defines exegesis as a "critical intepretation of a text or a portion of Scripture." Thus English and some other modern languages even use it as a special term for the critical interpretation of the Bible. For exegesis, though its tools and techniques are derived from classical philology, differs from philology,[39] because it is *philology plus.* And the *plus* is the presupposition of faith with which one employs the critical method.

Exegesis is concerned in the long run with the sense of the biblical passage in its final form: it seeks to draw out the meaning of the passage expressed by the inspired writer. This includes not only the *textual meaning* (the sense of its words and phrases—what the medievals meant by the "literal" sense), but also its *contextual meaning* (the sense of the words or phrases in a given passage or episode, a unit of the text), and its *relational meaning* (their sense in relation to the book or the corpus of works as a whole). The last meaning, the relational, is sometimes called its biblical-theological meaning, because it seeks to interpret the words and phrases according to the synthesis of ideas of the biblical writer. This combination of the textual, contextual, and relational meanings of a

---

[38] Along with *diorthōsis* (textual criticism), *anagnōsis* (reading), and *krisis* (criticism), *exēgēsis* (exposition of the text) formed part of ancient Alexandrian philological study. See H. I. Marrou, *History* (n. 3 above), 165–69.

[39] See S. Brown, "Philology," *The New Testament and Its Modern Interpreters* (ed. E. J. Epp and G. W. MacRae; Atlanta, GA: Scholars, 1989) 127–47.

passage amounts to its theological or religious meaning, to its meaning as the Word of God couched in ancient human language, and to the inspired message that accosts the reader of today.

With such a plus or presupposition of faith the modern Catholic interpreter of the Bible employs the philological tools and techniques of the historical-critical method in order to ascertain the textual, contextual, and relational meaning of a biblical passage or book. For the "plus" consists of elements of faith: that the book being critically interpreted contains God's Word set forth in human words of long ago; that it has been composed under the guidance of the Spirit and has therefore authority for the people of the Jewish-Christian heritage; that it is part of a restricted collection of authoritative ancient writings (part of a canon); that it has been given by God to His people for their edification and salvation; that the Spirit who inspired the authors of Scripture is the same as the Spirit who enables the community of interpreters and believers to read and understand its inspired text; that in it and through it God Himself continues to speak to human readers of every generation of His people; and that it is properly expounded only in relation to the Tradition that has grown out of it within the communal faith-life of that people, i.e., within the communion of the Church.[40]

What ultimately lies behind a faith-accompanied critical reading of Scripture in the Church is the conviction that God's revelation to His people took place *in the past*, both before and in Jesus Christ, and that the record of that self-manifestation of God is disclosed to the Church through Christ Jesus in the Bi-

---

[40] In effect, this is to agree with K. Barth's concept of "pneumatic" exegesis, even though one might hesitate to agree with his skepticism about human reason and his analysis of the relation of the Bible to the Church. See his *Church Dogmatics* (14 vols.; Edinburgh: Clark, 1956–77) 1/1, 183.

ble, in the Word of God couched in ancient human wording. This is the basic reason why historical criticism of the Bible has played and still has to play an important role in the life of the Church itself. This, however, does not deny the guidance and assistance of the Spirit in Church life. Yet that Spirit has never been conceived of as an ongoing revealer functioning somehow independently of Scripture. The Spirit has guided and continues to guide the Church through the centuries into a fuller and deeper understanding of the *historical* revelation once given to God's people before and in Jesus of Nazareth. As the Fourth Evangelist has put on the lips of Jesus, "The Paraclete, the holy Spirit, whom the Father will send in my name, will teach you all things and will remind you of all that I have said to you" (John 14:25); "when the Spirit of Truth comes, He will guide you into all truth, for he will not speak on his own authority" (16:13). Through that fuller understanding of the historical revelation given by the Spirit God speaks to Christians of today. Yet what he says to Christians of today in that fuller understanding is not wholly different from the primary revelation conveyed to the people of God of old. The homogeneity of God's revelation is sacrosanct.

Because the historical-critical method is per se neutral, it can be used with such faith presuppositions. Indeed, by reason of them it becomes a *properly-oriented* method of biblical interpretation, for none of the elements of the method is pursued in and for itself. It is a method that is not perfect, and because it is practised by so many interpreters, it is not surprising that their reconstructions of the past or their assessment of the meaning of the ancient texts is not necessarily uniform or unanimously agreed upon. Yet the techniques, when properly employed, are used only to achieve the main goal of discerning what the biblical message was that the sacred writer of long ago sought to convey and what it continues to say to readers today. As a neutral method, it can still undergo refinements in its his-

torical or literary aspects. New approaches in biblical interpretation are proposed from time to time, some of them claiming to be of a "post-critical" character,[41] some of them serving
to correct and refine the basic method itself.

IV. *Problems*

The historical-critical method, however, has in recent
times been criticized. It is said to be defective, to be based on
a false premise (reason alone), to be claiming a certitude similar to that of the natural sciences, to be fixated on hypothetical documents rather than on the actual biblical text, to be
dissecting the biblical text to the point that its literary unity
can no longer be appreciated, and to be lacking all interest in
the religious message of the Bible and its contemporary relevance for the spiritual lives of those who would read it today.

These are serious criticisms, said to proceed from theological considerations. They have been summarized by S.
Scherrer, who writes, "The historical-critical method, as it has
been predominantly practiced, is based on the *false premise*
that an *adequate* interpretation of Scripture, for the use of the
Church, can be made by basing its key exegetical decisions on
reason alone."[42]

---

[41] See D. Farkasfalvy, "In Search of a 'Post-Critical' Method of Biblical Interpretation for Catholic Theology," *Communio / International Catholic Review* 13
(1986) 288–307; A. C. Outler, "Toward a Postliberal Hermeneutics," *TToday* 42
(1985–86) 281–96.

[42] See "The Lord of History and Historical Criticism," *SJP News* (Maryknoll,
NY: St. Jerome Publications) 1/2 (1992) 1–6, esp. 2 (his italics). Cf. his "Biblical
Studies: Where Did We Go Wrong?" *SJP News* 1/3 (1992) 1–5; "Is the Historical-
Critical Method in Biblical Studies Bankrupt?" *SJP News* 1/1 (1992 [appeared Feb-
ruary 1993]) 1–5; "Fanciful Reconstructions of the Historical-Critical Method; and
the Historic Biblical Revelation of Salvation History," *SJP News* 2/2 (1993) 1–9;
"Criticizing the Bible? Where Ought We Now Go in Biblical Studies?" *SJP* 2/4 (1993)
1–4. Cf. also M. J. Wrenn, "Contemporary Catholic Biblical Scholarship: Certitudes

What may save such criticism from absurdity is the clause, "as it has been predominantly practiced." Although the historical-critical method has at times been practised in the way Scherrer asserts and there have been practitioners who have thought that their task was finished when they had laid bare the prehistory of a biblical book or its hypothetical sources or documents, which has led to their neglect of the actual biblical text and its religious message, this has not normally been the "predominant" aim of Christian interpreters who use the method, especially those in the Catholic Church. From M.-J. Lagrange on, most of the great exegetes in the church in recent decades have not neglected the religious or theological message of the written Word of God in their use of the historical-critical method and have not based their key exegetical decisions on reason alone.[43]

Scherrer has at least recognized that Raymond E.

---

or Hypotheses?" *Kecharitōmenē: Mélanges René Laurentin* (Paris: Desclée, 1990) 85–101.

[43] Scherrer criticizes R. de Vaux and his use of this method. According to him, it enables de Vaux to regard the account in 1 Chr 21:29; 16:39–40; 2 Chr 1:3–6 about "the one altar built by Moses and residing in Gibeon at the time of David and Solomon" as a "falsification" and the tradition about a single sanctuary where the people of Israel were to worship Yahweh as "late and unreliable" (*SJP News* 1/2 [1992] 4). De Vaux did use the adjective "late," but he did not call the statement false or unreliable. In fairness, one must consider what de Vaux was discussing and how he was discussing it. He was not writing a commentary on 1–2 Chronicles; nor was he trying to bring out the religious meaning of such biblical texts. The book to which Scherrer refers is de Vaux's classic treatment of the institutions of ancient Israel. The full title of this highly-regarded book is *Ancient Israel: Its Life and Institutions* (New York: McGraw-Hill, 1961).

Moreover, one must ask whether the tradition about the one sanctuary where Israel was to worship Yahweh and its location in Jerusalem is an example of a "truth," which "the books of Scripture" teach "firmly, faithfully, and without error" and which "God wanted put into the sacred writings for the sake of our salvation," as the Second Vatican Council taught about the inerrancy of the sacred text (*Dei verbum* §11). De Vaux's position is not "in *open* contradiction to the *explicit religious* teaching of the sacred text!" (Scherrer's italics). The religious teaching of that text—about

Brown, who has made use of the historical-critical method and has stoutly defended it,[44] practises what he (Scherrer) calls "a very *pure* type of exegesis, which seems to be becoming rarer and rarer these days." Yet he tries to maintain that Brown's exegesis and what he has been criticizing are "not exactly the same thing," and that "the majority in the field are moving farther and farther away from Fr. Brown's personal . . . way of doing Biblical scholarship within a Church setting."[45] The trouble here is that Scherrer is making an invalid distinction. Brown's mode of interpreting Scripture is a good example of the way the historical-critical method is *properly* practised, and Brown himself is not afraid to acknowledge his adherence to that method. Scherrer's wholesale criticism of the way the method "has been predominantly practiced" fails to countenance the diversity of presupposition with which the neutral method has been and is being employed.

Cardinal Ratzinger is cited by Scherrer as one who has

Israel's obligation to worship Yahweh—is intact in de Vaux's interpretation, whether or not the tradition about where the single sanctuary was to be located is late or not. Scherrer has not shown that the locality or the lateness of the tradition is part of the explicit *religious* teaching of Scripture.

There is another problem in Scherrer's criticism and his reference to "reason alone," which stands in contrast to a recommendation of Leo XIII himself in *Providentissimus Deus*. The Pope acknowledged that the use of human reason also had a place in biblical interpretation: "But he [the exegete] must not on that account consider that it is forbidden, when just cause exists, to push inquiry and exposition beyond what the Fathers have done; provided he carefully observes the rule so wisely laid down by St. Augustine—not to depart from the literal and obvious sense, except only *where reason makes it untenable* or necessity requires" (§112 [emphasis added]). Leo refers to Augustine, *De Gen. ad litt.* 8.7.13 [*nisi qua eum vel ratio tenere prohibeat vel necessitas cogat dimittere*]).

[44] See, e.g., "Historical-Critical Exegesis and Attempts at Revisionism," *The Bible Today* 23/3 (1985) 157–65.

[45] *SJP News* 1/3 (1993) 3.

also critized modern biblical criticism.[46] With him Scherrer associates B. S. Childs, J. A. Sanders, P. Stuhlmacher, H. Boers, Protestant critics of the method as well.[47] When the criticism of modern exegesis comes from Card. Ratzinger, that implies that he would include Catholic interpreters, because his criticism is hardly addressed solely to those outside the Church. Moreover, Card. Ratzinger does not find fault with the method only because of what some of its practitioners do with it, but maintains that "its erroneous application is due to the defects of the method itself. . . . [I]t contains such

---

[46] See "Biblical Interpretation in Crisis" (n. 37 above), 1–23. When Card. Ratzinger gave this paper as the Erasmus Lecture in New York, three other papers formed part of the program: "The Contribution of Historical Biblical Criticism to Ecumenical Church Discussion," by R. E. Brown (pp. 24–49); "Luther's 'Sola Scriptura': Traditions of the Gospel for Norming Christian Righteousness," by W. H. Lazareth (pp. 50–73); and "Scripture, Consensus, and Community," by George Lindbeck (pp. 74–101). In the same publication there is also an account of the discussion on this occasion, "The Story of an Encounter," by P. T. Stallsworth (pp. 102–90).
Another form of these lectures can be found in the German version, *Schriftauslegung im Widerstreit* (QD 117; ed. J. Ratzinger; Freiburg im B.: Herder, 1989). It gives a German version of the four lectures only, with no report of the discussions. In studying these lectures, one should consult J. Wicks, "Biblical Criticism Criticized," *Gregorianum* 72 (1991) 117–28; P. Grelot, Review of the English title, *RB* 98 (1991) 443–48.
[47] See B. S. Childs, *Introduction to the Old Testament as Scripture* (Philadelphia, PA: Fortress, 1978); *The New Testament as Canon: An Introduction* (Philadelphia, PA: Fortress, 1984); J. A. Sanders, *From Sacred Story to Sacred Text* (Philadelphia, PA: Fortress, 1987); P. Stuhlmacher, *Historical Criticism and Theological Interpretation of Scripture: Toward a Hermeneutics of Consent* (Philadelphia, PA: Fortress, 1977); H. Boers, "Historical Criticism versus Prophetic Proclamation," *HTR* 65 (1972) 393–414.
Cf. R. W. Klein, "The Childs' Proposal: A Symposium with Ralph W. Klein, Gary Stansell and Walter Brueggemann," *Word & World* 1 (1981) 105–15; K. Froehlich, "Biblical Hermeneutics on the Move," *Word & World* 1 (1981) 140–52; C. Davis, "The Theological Career of Historical Criticism of the Bible," *Cross Currents* 32 (1982–83) 267–84; E. Lindemann, *Historical Criticism of the Bible: Methodology or Ideology?* (Grand Rapids, MI: Baker, 1990).

significant mistaken assumptions that a reexamination of it is now incumbent upon all who would affirm the perennial importance of God's written word for the church and for the world of today."[48] As a result Card. Ratzinger calls for, not a return to the patristic-medieval approach, but an examination of the approach epitomized by Dibelius and Bultmann, and for the development of a new method, which will preserve the strengths of both approaches but will be cognizant of the shortcomings of both.

My earlier presentation of the historical-critical method has already implicitly answered some of these objections. In insisting on the neutrality of the method in itself, in rejecting the presuppositions, rationalist, antidogmatic, or philosophical, with which it has at times been used but with which it

---

[48] These words are not found in the Cardinal's paper itself but are attributed to him in P. T. Stallsworth's "The Story of an Encounter," *Biblical Interpretation in Crisis* (nn. 37 and 46 above) 104. There Ratzinger is said to have summarized his position by listing three such mistaken assumptions: (1) that the historical-critical method "enjoys a degree of certitude similar to that enjoyed by the natural sciences"; it fails to realize that Scripture belongs to an area of investigation that is not subject to strict scientific calculation (104); (2) that it presupposes a discontinuity, according to which "the understanding of Jesus prevalent in one phase does not necessarily continue into the next phase" (105); and (3) that "the influence of the history of religions school" and its affirmation of "an objective, scientific methodology" as "an absolute rule for distinguishing between what could have been and what should be explained by developments" are to be explained "on a deeper level" with a philosophical presupposition of Kant. "According to him, it is only through practical reason that man can make contact with the reality that is his destiny. But using his empirical categories of exact science by definition excludes the appearance of the One who is 'Wholly Other' and the initiative of that One (106)." Hence how is one to show any real relevance of Jesus for life today?

By contrast, Ratzinger insisted on three things: (1) "Theology—the study of God and God's relationship with humanity—cannot be confused with the natural sciences" (106); (2) one has to "learn from the extraordinary," that something without precedent may occur in history; hence one need not renounce Christian faith to read Scripture; and (3) "the relationship between word and event" must be reexamined, because in accord with biblical terminology "the event itself can be word" (107).

need not be used, and in stressing the presupposition of faith with which most Catholic interpreters normally employ the method, I have tried to show how it can be properly utilized.

Surprisingly, Card. Ratzinger, in aiming his remarks at modern interpreters, cites the example of Dibelius and Bultmann in his analysis of the crisis, as if all recent interpreters of Scripture, Catholic and non-Catholic alike, were still working with the liberal approach of Dibelius or the radical skepticism of Bultmann, admitting in their work the Bultmannian subordination of the event to the word, or using the philosophy of Heidegger or Kant in their interpretation.[49] As the Lutheran New Testament scholar Karl Paul Donfried put it, "Historical-critical scholarship has come a long way since the days of the Bultmannian hegemony."[50]

What such critics of the historical-critical method do not tell us is what mode of post-critical interpretation one is to use as a substitute for historical criticism. All too frequently they espouse a form of literal interpretation not far removed from the fundamentalist, even though they may reject such a label for the interpretation that they are advocating, or take refuge in some other senses of Scripture, patristic, spiritual, or otherwise.

Yet it must be recalled that it was precisely in reaction to

---

[49] Having shown the dependence of the Dibelius-Bultmann approach on Kantian philosophy and its explanation that what might "seem like a direct proclamation of the divine can only be myth," Ratzinger in his paper goes on to say: "It is with this basic conviction that Bultmann, *with the majority of modern exegetes*, read the Bible. He is certain that it cannot be the way it is depicted in the Bible, and he looks for methods to prove the way it really had to be. To that extent there lies in modern exegesis a reduction of history into philosophy, a revision of history by means of philosophy. . . . At its core, the debate about modern exegesis is not a dispute among historians: it is rather a philosophical debate" ("Biblical Interpretation in Crisis," 16 [my italics]).

[50] Donfried so answered Card. Ratzinger's claim during the discussion at the Conference; see P. Stallsworth's report, *Biblical Interpretation* (n. 46 above), 111.

the medieval multiple senses of Scripture that the historical-critical method of interpretation came into renewed use in its quest of the meaning expressed by the human author. Reaction to the allegorical use of Scripture was particularly strong at the time of the Renaissance, the Reformation, and the Enlightenment,[51] and it is this heritage with which we have to live in the Church of the twentieth century.

---

[51] Here one should recall the ancient roots of the historical-critical method (see pp. 8–14), which both Scherrer and Card. Ratzinger obfuscate. See *SJP News* 1/2 (1992) 2, col. 2. The cardinal is quoted as speaking of Dibelius and Bultmann as the ones "who devised the method" (*Biblical Interpretation in Crisis*, 104). As a matter of fact, Dibelius and Bultmann *added* to the method itself, as used of the New Testament, the refinement of form criticism. Bultmann in particular also linked to his use of the method so refined certain hermeneutical presuppositions, philosophical and demythologizing. Neither the method nor the refinement of form criticism, however, is at fault, as the Instruction of the Biblical Commission of 1964 recognized (pars. V, X), but the Bultmannian presuppositions were, and today they are seen by many, many interpreters, as unacceptable.

2. OTHER APPROACHES TO THE UNDERSTANDING OF SCRIPTURE

Numerous approaches to the reading and interpretation of the Bible have been advocated in recent decades. One hears of the new literary criticism, of narrative criticism, rhetorical criticism, canonical criticism, sociological interpretation, anthropological interpretation, psychological interpretation, structuralist criticism, feminist criticism, and so on. Obviously, not all of them are of equal value. I shall comment only on those I consider of importance: (I) new literary criticism; (II) narrative approach; (III) rhetorical approach; (IV) canonical approach; (V) sociological approach; (VI) psychological approach; and (VII) feminist approach.

I refer to them as approaches, because none of them is a method of interpretation complete in itself or one that can rival or be substituted for the basic historical-critical method. They are approaches to the biblical text, however, that may correct certain tendencies of the basic method or refine it in specific directions.

I. *New Literary Criticism*

The first of such approaches is the new literary criticism. As applied to the Bible, it has had the advantage of making readers aware that, in perusing it, they are indeed reading one of the great masterpieces of world literature. For the Bible, even apart from its sacred character and religious value for Jews and Christians, has been reckoned as one of the great books of literature. This does not mean, of course, that every part of the Bible would be so regarded, but certain parts have always been acknowledged as outstanding in literary quality, and as a whole it is rightly so recognized.

The new literary approach to the Bible seeks to treat it as one does other masterpieces of world literature, regarding the biblical text as an autonomous entity. According to this approach, the biblical text, once consigned to writing, is said to take on a life of its own, independent of the historical setting from which it emerged. Then it is analyzed according to its literary techniques. What might have been the original intention of the human author becomes unimportant, and the biblical text is sometimes regarded as conveying meaning scarcely envisaged by the author. What is important is the world of the text, a perception of reality which the text takes on in its continued existence, and its assumption into the canon. Parallels to biblical forms and genres are often sought in other world literature, shedding light on the function of Old and New Testament poetry, rhetoric, narratives, wisdom sayings, epistles, etc.[1]

Some modern advocates of this form of literary study of

---

[1] See, for example, R. Alter and F. Kermode (eds.), *The Literary Guide to the Bible* (Cambridge, MA: Belknap Press, Harvard University, 1987). When one uses this guide, one should not overlook the amount of material in it that has been borrowed from standard introductions to the Bible written according to the historical-critical method. Even such a literary guide to the Bible has had to depend on the sure results of that method. Cf. also N. Frye, *The Great Code: The Bible and Literature* (New York/London: Harcourt Brace Jovanovich, 1982); *Anatomy of Criticism* (Princeton, NJ: Princeton University, 1957); L. Alonso Schökel, "Hermeneutical Problems of a Literary Study of the Bible," *Congress Volume, Edinburgh 1974* (VTSup 28; Leiden: Brill, 1975) 1–15; *The Inspired Word: Scripture in the Light of Language and Literature* (New York: Herder and Herder, 1965).

the Bible give the impression that literary analysis of the Bible has been overlooked. In their opinion, literary criticism is superior to and even of greater importance than the historical or the theological approach to the Bible.[2] Now perhaps some of the refined techniques of this new criticism have not been used to the extent that they might and can be adopted in a sound interpretation of the Bible, but it must be remembered that a literary approach to the Bible has always been part of the historical-critical method itself.[3]

Moreover, this new criticism runs the risk of absolutizing its literary character. T. S. Eliot, a littérateur in his own right, once assessed such literary criticism of the Bible:

> While I acknowledge the legitimacy of this enjoyment, I am more acutely aware of its abuse. The persons who enjoy these writings *solely* because of their literary merit are essentially parasites; and we know that parasites, when they become too numerous, are pests. I could fulminate against the men of letters who have gone into ecstasies over 'the Bible as literature,' the Bible as 'the noblest monument of English prose.' Those who talk of the Bible as a 'monument of English prose' are merely admiring it as a monument over the grave of Christianity. I must try to avoid the by-paths of my discourse: it is enough to suggest that just as the work of Clarendon, or Gibbon, or Buffon, or Bradley would be of inferior literary value if it were insignificant as history, science and philosophy respectively, so the Bible has had a *literary* influence upon English literature *not* because it has been considered as liter-

---

[2] See D. Robertson, "Literature, The Bible as," *IDBSup*, 547–51: "These scholars, who come from diverse philosophical and theological traditions, are united in considering the Bible primarily and fundamentally as a literary document (as opposed, e.g., to considering it as a historical or theological document)" (p. 547).

[3] See pp. 20–21 above.

ature, but because it has been considered as the report of the Word of God. And the fact that men of letters now discuss it as literature probably indicates the *end* of its 'literary' influence.[4]

Another difficulty perceived in this approach is its tendency to regard the biblical text as autonomous, that it can take on a meaning of its own independent of that of the author's intention. Although one can understand how a secular poem (for instance, a Shakespearean sonnet) might assume such autonomy and can be shown to have taken on a meaning that its author never dreamed of, a meaning that is also quite important, that explanation is hardly applicable to the written Word of God without further ado. Given the inspiration of the Bible, it is rather of supreme importance that the meaning of the Bible in the twentieth century have a homogeneity with that originally intended by the human author inspired by God to record His Word. The biblical text cannot take on such an autonomous character or meaning as this new critical approach to the Bible may assume. But more on this later on.[5]

One must also recall that in the United States this approach to the Bible has often been supported by an extrinsic consideration, by the creation of departments of religious studies in state universities, departments in which many religions are studied on an equal basis, and their sacred writings treated as examples of religious literature. As a result, this sort

---

[4] *Selected Essays: New Edition* (New York: Harcourt, Brace, 1950) 344–45 (his italics).

[5] See further F. Neirynck, "Literary Criticism, Old and New," *The Synoptic Gospels: Source Criticism and the New Literary Criticism* (BETL 110; ed. C. Focant; Louvain: Leuven University/Peeters, 1993), 11–38; J. Barr, "Reading the Bible as Literature," *BJRL* 56 (1973-74) 10–33; "Story and History in Biblical Theology," *JR* 56 (1976) 1–17; repr. in *The Scope and Authority of the Bible* (Philadelphia, PA: Westminster, 1980) 1–17.

of literary interpretation of the Bible tends to forget that Scripture finds its real matrix and function in a faith-community: the Old Testament is the reflection of the faith of the community of Israel; the New Testament along with the Old is the Church's book. Hence the implication that the Bible can be understood in some literary way that prescinds from its faith-community context is misguided.

This literary approach to the Bible is also responsible at times for the non-canonical approach to it that is advocated in some university-milieux.

Two specific recent developments in the literary approach to the Bible may now be mentioned: the narrative approach and the rhetorical approach.

II. *Narrative Approach*

The narrative approach concentrates on the communicative power of biblical stories as a means of transmitting the Word of God.[6] Realizing that people often pass on a message or make an argumentative point by telling a story, interpreters who use this technique seek to reckon with the Bible as significantly communicating God's Word through his deeds presented in narrative accounts: stories, with plots, characters, and dénouements. Thus the Old Testament has many accounts of God's salvific activity on behalf of his people, and

---

[6] See J.-N. Aletti, "L'Approccio narrativo applicato alla Bibbia: Stato della questione e proposte," *RivB* 39 (1991) 257–76. Cf. R. Alter, *The Art of Biblical Narrative* (New York: Basic Books, 1981); H. W. Frei, *The Eclipse of Biblical Narrative: A Study in Eighteenth and Nineteenth Century Hermeneutics* (New Haven/London: Yale University, 1974); K. R. R. Gros Louis, et al. (eds.), *Literary Interpretation of Biblical Narratives* (The Bible in Literature Courses; Nashville, TN: Abingdon, 1974); M. Weiss, "Einiges über die Bauformen des Erzählens in der Bibel," *VT* 13 (1963) 456–75; "Weiteres über die Bauformen des Erzählens in der Bibel," *Bib* 46 (1965) 181–206.

this salvation history is even summarized in catechetical résumés (e.g., Ps 78:3–4). The New Testament, especially in its gospel stories and in the Acts of the Apostles, recollects and presents narratives of the ministry, passion, death, and resurrection of Jesus Christ and of their sequel, as the early Christian Church emerged. In effect, it is a recounting of "the story of the cross" (1 Cor 1:18). And even the letters of the Pauline corpus can be analyzed for their narrative substructures, their implied tales about God's activity with His new people fashioned by the story of Jesus itself. Thus from beginning to end the Bible is seen to have a basically narrative character, which accosts the reader with its story-form, and even in a symbolic way.[7]

Such an approach brings out an aspect of the communicated Word of God that had at times been neglected in the traditional literary criticism of the Bible, but it is not universally applicable, despite the allegations of some of its practitioners. For much of the written Word of God is simply not cast in narrative form, and the message of the stories, which are alleged to be the substructure of the rest, comes through in greatly watered-down form. The prophetic and wisdom literature of the Old Testament and much of the epistolary writings of the New Testament would be inadequate objects of such analysis. As P. Perkins has noted,

> . . . the plurality of readings which narrative criticism suggests frustrates what may be the most pervasive goal of theological readings of Scripture: to fix the meaning of the text, to compel it to make an authoritative pronounce-

---

[7] See D. Rhoads and D. Michie, *Mark as Story: An Introduction to the Narrative of a Gospel* (Philadelphia, PA: Fortress, 1982); J. D. Kingsbury, *Matthew as Story* (Philadelphia, PA: Fortress, 1986). Cf. J. B. Metz, *Faith in History and Society* (New York: Seabury/Crossroad, 1980) 205–18, esp. 212–13.

ment on some issues of theological or ethical concern.
. . . Narrative analysis does not yield the kind of conceptual syntheses which might provide the introductory paragraphs to systematic expositions of Christology, ecclesiology, Christian discipleship, or ethics. . . . In the Christian tradition our stories have provoked theological and ethical reflection, but they do not hand us theology or ethics on a platter ready for consumption.[8]

Yet certain aspects of the narrative approach could offer a refinement of the basic historical-critical method itself.

III. *Rhetorical Approach*

The rhetorical approach to the Bible, however, would be more relevant, since its aim is to analyze the persuasive character of Scripture, the techniques and devices used to accost the readers and to arouse in them proper reactions, emotions, values, and interests. Because it is the written Word of God with an edifying and kerygmatic purpose, Scripture contains many elements of ancient rhetorical writing.[9] It is a body of literature composed in view of a persuasive goal. Moreover, this rhetorical approach to the Bible not only studies those elements, but it also presses beyond the form-critical analysis of small units in seeking with rhetorical analysis to determine the message of a biblical writing as a whole. It is particularly suited to the study of the biblical text because the written

---

[8] "Crisis in Jerusalem? Narrative Criticism in New Testament Studies," *TS* 50 (1989) 296–313, esp. 312–13.

[9] See A. N. Wilder, *Early Christian Rhetoric* (London: SCM, 1964; Cambridge, MA: Harvard University, 1971); G. A. Kennedy, *New Testament Interpretation through Rhetorical Criticism* (Chapel Hill, NC: University of North Carolina, 1984); Clines, D. J. A. et al. (eds), *Art and Meaning: Rhetoric in Biblical Literature* (JSOTSup 19; Sheffield, UK: University of Sheffield, 1982).

Word of God seeks to secure allegiance, loyalty, and faith. In other words, it seeks to convince or to explain, and thus makes use of many ancient rhetorical devices. The authority of the orator (= the author), the discourse he utters (= the text), and the audience addressed (= the readers) can all be analyzed duly from a rhetorical point of view in the effort to bring out the proper emotional response. All three forms of ancient rhetorical eloquence have been found in the Bible: judiciary, deliberative, and demonstrative, i.e., the kind of rhetoric used in law-courts, political assemblies, and popular celebrations. Such rhetorical analysis, based on the classical rhetoric of the Greco-Latin tradition, however, would have to be supplemented with elements of Semitic rhetoric that are also found in the Bible: symmetric composition, parallelism. All in all, this new rhetorical approach to the Bible has sought to exploit the power of persuasive communication in a given sociological structure.

Obviously, much in this approach can enrich the classic historical-critical method, which in its literary aspect has not always exploited the rhetorical potential of the biblical text, especially in its sapiential, ethical, and communitarian parts. The hortatory sections of Pauline letters could well profit from a better rhetorical analysis. And yet, even though some proponents propagate this analysis as a substitute for the historical-critical method, it is not clearly a substitute for it. Joined to the latter, however, it can have great advantage, because it would ensure that the basic method is not lost merely in historical analysis, but would seek to direct that analysis along rhetorical lines to the comprehension of the biblical text as a whole.

IV. *Canonical Approach*

Still another technique of recent proposal has been canonical criticism, which not only considers a biblical book in its final form, but also as it functions within the whole of

Scripture.[10] Thus one can consider the biblical text as it came to be written: from its oral-tradition stage through its scribal compilation, editing, and selection process, as well as the ongoing meaning that a given written text, once incorporated into a canon, develops within such a collection as a record and witness of the faith of a community. This mode of interpretation enables the interpreter to consider the process whereby older traditions are adapted to new religious and cultural situations. Especially important is the way the New Testament picks up and quotes or uses the Old Testament, its traditions as well as its wording. But there are also examples of rereading within the Old Testament itself, for instance, when the Exodus tradition is utilized to enhance the account of God's guidance of Israel in its return from the Babylonian Captivity. It thus emphasizes the theocentric aspect of Scripture, as it depicts God acting as creator and savior of his world and his people in spite of their rebellion against him. Moreover, it accords to Scripture its proper *Sitz im Leben*, viz. in the communities of faith.

Such an analysis of Scripture, important though it is, is dependent, however, on the canon concerned, whether it be the Jewish canon, the Protestant canon, the Catholic canon, or the Orthodox canon. Yet the principle would be the same in each case, because it would seek to interpret biblical pas-

---

[10] Here one would have to distinguish the approach of J. A. Sanders, *Torah and Canon* (Philadelphia, PA: Fortress, 1972); *Canon and Community: A Guide to Canonical Criticism* (Philadelphia, PA: Fortress, 1984); "Biblical Criticism and the Bible as Canon," *USQR* 32 (1976–77) 157–65; "Text and Canon: Concepts and Method," *JBL* 98 (1979) 5–29, and that of B. S. Childs, *Introduction to the Old Testament as Scripture* (Philadelphia, PA: Fortress, 1978; *The New Testament as Canon: An Introduction* (Philadelphia, PA: Fortress, 1984). Cf. R. W. Klein, "The Childs' Proposal: A Symposium with Ralph W. Klein, Gary Stansell and Walter Brueggemann," *Word & World* 1 (1981) 105–15; R. P. Carroll, "Canonical Criticism: A Recent Trend in Biblical Studies?" *ExpTim* 92 (1980–81) 73–78.

sages within given corpora of the Word of God for different faith communities, along with their traditions.

Whether one should call this approach to Scripture a form of "criticism" is problematic, because it really does not take its place on the same level with source criticism, form criticism, redaction criticism, narrative criticism, or rhetorical criticism, all of which tell us something about the process by which a biblical book came to be and reached its final form. In a sense, this mode of interpretation might be called post-biblical, because it says much more about the after-effects of biblical books, about the relationship of fully-constituted biblical writings to one another, and how they function in the whole collection, than about the individual texts in their process of growth or in the attainment of their final form. It is true, however, that the Old Testament canon might be seen as a collection having a corporate influence on the New Testament and individual New Testament writings in their very compilation and composition, as they were affected by Old Testament passages.[11] But there is a problem in that one may not be able to speak of a closed canon of Old Testament books prior to the writing of New Testament. Again, which Jewish canon is to be considered? The Palestinian or the Alexandrian, the Hebrew or the Greek? Moreover, one cannot ignore the influence that extracanonical Jewish writings, or so-called intertestamental Jewish literature, have had on New Testament compositions.[12] Again, canonical criticism tells us little about the meaning of early writings of the Old Testament in themselves, even though such early writings assume a further significance once they have found themselves in a collection of later date, whether Palestinian or Alexandrian. This ap-

---

[11] For example, the role that the Book of Wisdom played in Paul's discussion of pagans without the gospel in Rom 1:18–32.

[12] For example, the quotation of *1 Enoch* 18:15–16 in Jude 14.

proach to Scripture is clearly important for theology, and more will be said about its importance in due time, but another problem has to be mentioned now.

This problem arises from the fact that both Jews and Christians read the Hebrew Scriptures or the Old Testament and feed their religious lives on it, and that both Jews and Christians, in doing so, often employ the historical-critical method of interpretation. This would seem to imply that Jews and Christians should be able to agree on the meaning of a passage of the Hebrew Scriptures in and for itself, even though both would relate such a passage to a different canon, and a different after-life (or tradition). For a Jewish interpreter the famous dictum of Augustine, *In Vetere Novum (Testamentum) latet, et in Novo Vetus patet,*[13] would, of course, mean nothing, but even the Christian interpreter has to be careful in interpreting the Old Testament, not to make it carry only the sense of *praeparatio evangelica.* The religious or theological sense of the Old Testament is something that Jewish interpreters would be supremely interested in, and that sense is per se what Christian interpreters should be able to agree on with them,[14] even though Christians might further see a plus value, which comes to Old Testament passages because of their place

---

[13] *Quaestiones in Heptateuchum* 2.73; CSEL 28/3/3. 141.

[14] See further R. E. Murphy, "The Fear of the Lord: A Fear to End All Fears," *Overcoming Fear between Jews and Christians* (ed. J. H. Charlesworth et al.; The American Interfaith Institute; New York: Crossroad, 1992) 172–80, esp. 173–74: ". . . the achievement of modern scholarship is such that Christians and Jews have learned to interpret the Hebrew Bible on its own terms. Here there is much common ground where scholars must learn from one another and where Christians and Jews can stand together." And in n. 4 Murphy adds: "The common ground to which I refer is the interpretation of the Hebrew Bible according to historico-critical methodology. I readily grant that this methodology only approximates its goal of establishing the historical meaning, and also that it does not exhaust the meaning of the text. With all its limitations, however, it does succeed in establishing a shared understanding that is ecumenically important."

in a Christian canon and because they are read in light of the Christ-event.

V. *Sociological Approach*

Another recent development in biblical interpretation is the *sociological approach*. This development presses beyond the form-critical interest, which sought to determine the communitarian *Sitz im Leben* of a given gospel form, into a much broader analysis that utilizes techniques derived from social sciences, especially from sociology and cultural anthropology, to analyze the traces of social interaction within the people of God and the traces of ancient societal life, Palestinian or Hellenistic, which are reflected in the Bible.[15]

Most of the Bible represents not theological treatises, but rather documents that have emerged from vital situations in God's people. These are marked by familial, societal, agrarian, urban, economic, and political concerns. At times, even different social and economic strata are reflected in the biblical text (e.g., in the kind of life led by Jesus, a wandering preacher, and by those to whom he preached; in the difference among Corinthian Christians in their celebration of the Eu-

---

[15] It is customary to refer to the sociological work of the German scholars Max Weber (*Ancient Judaism* [Glencoe, IL: Free Press, 1952]) and A. Deissmann (*Light from the Ancient East* (2d ed.; London: Hodder and Stoughton, 1927) and, among Americans, to the so-called Chicago School of interpretation, represented by S. J. Case, S. Mathews, and F. Grant. More recent forms of sociological interpretation have been proposed by G. Theissen, *Sociology of Early Palestinian Christianity* (Philadelphia, PA: Fortress, 1978); *The Social Setting of Pauline Christianity* (Philadelphia, PA: Fortress, 1982); J. H. Neyrey, *An Ideology of Revolt; John's Christology in Social-Science Perspective* (Philadelphia, PA: Fortress, 1988).

For the anthropological approach, see B. Lang (ed.), *Anthropological Approaches to the Old Testament* (Issues in Religion and Theology 8; Philadelphia, PA: Fortress, 1985).

charist; in the attitude toward slavery and the nuance that it provides for Paul's use of *doulos*, even when applied to Christians). The social world in which the people of the Old and New Testament lived, together with their customs and institutions, their functions and status, thus often impinges on the meaning of the sacred text itself.

This sociological approach offers to the historical-critical method an enrichment, but it is scarcely a substitute for that method. The elements of the social world of the ancient people who appear in the Bible are not the *object* of the biblical writings themselves; they are at most reflected in it indirectly. Hence this approach to the Bible tends to read between the lines, and not the lines themselves. It can elucidate only an aspect of the record of the Word of God. But it normally does not seek to explain it in and for itself, nor can it. Moreover, sociological theory is not one. There are many schools of sociological analysis and expression, and the move from a modern sociological theory, which has per se been developed from living subjects in a given society, to that of an ancient people known only in part from written records creates a problem that cannot be glossed over.

VI. *Psychological Approach*

Something similar would have to be said about the psychological approach to the Bible, whether one considers the Freudian analysis of Moses or the Jungian archetypal analysis of various biblical motifs. The psychological and psychoanalytical analyses of human experience have proven their worth in the area of religion and enable one to detect multidimensional aspects of the biblical message. In particular, this approach has been invaluable in the analytical explanation of biblical symbols, cultic rituals, sacrifice, legal prohibitions, and biblical tabus. Yet once again, there is no one psychological or psychoanalytic exegesis that can substitute for the properly oriented historical-critical method,[16] whereas the aid that can come from this approach to that method cannot be underestimated.

VII. *Feminist Approach*

Yet another recent development has been the *feminist approach* to the Bible, which actually began in the United States at the end of the nineteenth century,[17] but was renewed in the 1970s. This approach has emerged owing to the increasing number of women interpreters of the Bible in recent decades, as a result of the general emancipation of women in modern culture and of their struggle for equality with men. As an approach to the understanding of the Bible, this perspective has added an important dimension. For biblical exposition has suffered from a predominance of male interpreters. Yet this approach does not offer itself as a substitute for the historical-critical method. Normally, it makes wide use of this method, and it has succeeded in studying critically and afresh the portraits of women in the Bible, the strata of biblical society in which women often played prominent roles both in Israel and in the early Christian Church. Especially in the New Testament, it has brought into proper and equitable light the roles of all disciples of Jesus, male and female, of the apostles Andronicus and Junia.

---

[16] This has been seen already in the prime example of this mode of interpretation of the Bible, in the writings of E. Drewermann of Germany, very little of whose work has been translated into English.

[17] See E. Cady Stanton, *The Woman's Bible* (2 vols.; New York: European Publ. Co, 1885, 1898). Cf. A. Yarbro Collins (ed.), *Feminist Perspectives on Biblical Scholarship* (Biblical Scholarship in North America 10; Chico, CA: Scholars, 1985); *Women's Bible Commentary* (Louisville, KY: Westminster/John Knox, 1992).

Operative in this approach, however, are some questionable elements. First, a hermeneutic of suspicion, which maintains that, since history is usually written by those who win out, even the biblical record has been composed by male conquerors, and hence it does not tell the whole story. So one cannot trust the text; one has to read between the lines for historical truth. This hermeneutic of suspicion has led to various forms of the feminist approach, even to the radical rejection of the Bible. Yet even if one does not agree with that radical rejection, this hermeneutical approach tends to substitute for the revelation enshrined in the biblical text an imaginative reconstruction of historical reality—for instance, of the Jesus-movement—as the norm for Christian belief and practice, which is unacceptable.[18] Second, the feminist approach is sometimes questionable in its interpretation of some biblical passages, e.g., Gal 3:28, which affirms that "there is neither Jew nor Greek, there is neither slave nor free person, there is not male and female; for you are all one in Christ Jesus." That is an affirmation of equal status "in Christ Jesus," or as a Christian, but it says nothing about the political status of men and women in modern culture or even in the Church of today.

The upshot judgment about these modern approaches to Scripture is that some of them can well enhance the historical-critical method, correct its inadequacies, or enrich it, enabling it better to bring out the real sense of the Word of God in its textual, contextual, and relational meanings, yes, even in its spiritual sense. But that brings me to the the topic of my next chapter.

---

[18] Card. J. Ratzinger has said of it: "Materialist and feminist exegesis, whatever else may be said about them, do not even claim to be an understanding of the text itself in the manner in which it was originally intended. At best they may be seen as an expression of the view that the Bible's message is in and of itself inexplicable, or else that it is meaningless for life in today's world. In this sense, they are no longer interested in ascertaining the truth, but only in whatever will serve their own particular agendas" ("Biblical Interpretation in Crisis," [n. 37 in chap. 1], 5).

3. SCRIPTURE, THE SOURCE OF THEOLOGY

Our discussion thus far has treated Scripture as the Word of God couched in ancient human language, in human words that preserve for Christians of all generations a form of God's self-revelation to his chosen people, at first to the people of Israel and then to the new people fashioned in and through Jesus of Nazareth. As Christians in the twentieth century we read and study that Word of God as the nourishment of our spiritual lives. But we do not study it in a vacuum. We are members of a faith-community that feeds its spiritual life, indeed, on the written Word of God along with the Tradition that has been born of it and that has helped to fashion the understanding of that written record.

As a community, we also seek to understand the faith that we have inherited and that we profess. For this reason we are interested in theology, *fides quaerens intellectum*, the process whereby we reflect on the faith of the Church.[1] Such an attempt to understand Christian faith clearly emerges from the written Word of God itself. For this reason the Second Vatican Council echoed the medieval designation of Scripture as "the Sacred Page" (*sacra Pagina*) and said that it should be "the soul of sacred Theology" (*anima sacrae Theologiae*).[2]

---

[1] See H. M. Vroom, "Does Theology Presuppose Faith?" *SJT* 45 (1992) 145–63.

[2] *Dei verbum* §24. In the Council's decree on Priestly Formation, this idea is repeated: "In the study of sacred Scripture, which ought to be the soul of all theology

Scripture's role thus described is derived from the encyclical of Pope Leo XIII, *Providentissimus Deus*,[3] who spoke of Scripture as the animating or vivifying principle of the understanding of Christian faith. The Council further explained: "By scrutinizing in the light of faith all truth stored up in the mystery of Christ, theology is most powerfully strengthened and constantly rejuvenated by that [written] word" (*Dei verbum* §24).

Yet it is not *sola Scriptura* that functions as the vivifying principle, for the Council also insisted:

> sacred Tradition . . . and sacred Scripture of both the Old and the New Testament are like a mirror in which the pilgrim Church on earth looks at God, from whom it has received everything. . . . There exist a close connection and communication between sacred Tradition and sacred Scripture. For both of them, flowing from the same divine wellspring, in a certain way merge into a unity and tend toward the same end. For sacred Scripture is the word of God inasmuch as it is consigned to writing under the inspiration of the divine Spirit. To the successors of the apostles, sacred Tradition hands on in its full purity God's word, entrusted to the apostles by Christ the Lord and the Holy Spirit. Thus, led by the light of the Spirit of truth, these successors can in their preaching preserve this word of God faithfully, explain it, and make it more widely known. Consequently, it is not from sacred Scripture

---

(*Sacrae Scripturae studio, quae universae theologiae veluti anima esse debet*), students should be trained with special diligence" (*Optatam totius* 16; *AAS* 58 [1966] 723). A slightly different emphasis is found in the International Theological Commission's document, *De interpretatione dogmatum*, which says, *Sacrae Scripturae studium theologiae simul et omnis praedicationis sit anima*, "The study of Sacred Scripture should be the soul of theology, and likewise of all preaching" (*Gregorianum* 72 [1991] 5–37, esp. 24 [c.1.1]).

[3] *ASS* 26 (1893–94) 269–92, esp. p. 283; *EB* §114.

alone that the Church draws her certainty about everything which has been revealed. Both sacred Tradition and
sacred Scripture are to be accepted and venerated with the
same sense of devotion and reverence.

Sacred Tradition and sacred Scripture form one sacred deposit of the word of God, which is committed to
the Church (*Dei verbum* §8–10).

[The Church] has always regarded the Scriptures together with sacred Tradition as the supreme rule of faith,
and will ever do so (§21).

This unity, then, in which Scripture and Tradition coin-
here and reflect to us the Word of God, is the way through
which Scripture serves as the soul of theology, "the pure and
perennial source of spiritual life" (§21). But Scripture so understood is Scripture *interpreted*, for that Tradition which is
born of it is itself an interpretation of Scripture,[4] and this leads
us to the further discussion of the senses of sacred Scripture
and the role that they play in the Church's theology. On this
score, my remarks will be made under three headings: (I) the
literal sense of Scripture; (II) the spiritual sense of Scripture,
and (III) Scripture as related to theology within the Church.

I. *The Literal Sense of Scripture*

As we have already seen, the properly-oriented use of the
historical-critical method of interpreting Scripture is aimed at
ascertaining the meaning of the Word of God as it was originally expressed by the inspired human author. Pius XII did
not hesitate to call this the "literal sense,"[5] for this is directly

---

[4] See B. W. Anderson, "Tradition and Scripture in the Community of Faith," *JBL* 100 (1981) 5–21.

[5] *Divino afflante Spiritu* §23 (see p. 17 above).

the effect of the movement of the Spirit. In the literal sense one finds the expression of God revealing Himself to humanity. Yet Pius XII did not mean by it a literalist or fundamentalistic understanding of Scripture, a concentration on the "letter" of the text that would exclude figurative language, metaphorical expression, parables, ironic statements, or even anthropomorphic descriptions of God. Nor did he mean the "letter" of the text without regard of its contextual meaning, its relational meaning, or its form.

The misunderstanding of the literal sense of Scripture has taken many forms in the course of history. Origen, usually regarded as the great allegorizer of Scripture, was himself at times guilty of concentration on the letter of the text.[6]

More crucial today is the literalist reading of Scripture, a concentration on the letter of the Word called Fundamentalism. This mode of interpreting Scripture grew out of a concern for the literal sense that developed at the time of the Reformation. In the time of the Reformers the literal sense was preferred to the multiple and allegorical senses often employed in the Middle Ages. After the period of the Enlightenment insistence on the literal sense became a safeguard against liberal Protestant interpretations of the Bible. The name "fundamentalism" is traced directly to the American Bible Conference held at Niagara, N.Y. in 1895, at which conservative evangelical theologians issued "Five Points of Fundamentalism," by which they meant the verbal inerrancy of Scripture, the divinity of Christ, the virgin birth, the substitutionary theory of the atonement, and the bodily resurrection and second coming of Christ. When the fundamentalist form of reading

---

[6] See E. Klostermann, *Origenes, Eusthatius von Antiochien und Gregor von Nyssa über die Hexe von Endor* (KIT 83; Bonn: Marcus und Weber, 1912). Eustathius attacked Origen's literal interpretation of 1 Sam 28:3–25, about the witch of Endor, in which Origen sought to find an argument for the resurrection.

the Bible spread to other parts of the world, it developed other equally-literalist forms, especially in Europe, Asia, Africa, and South America. Within the Catholic Church it has found adherents too, especially in the latter part of the twentieth century.

Though fundamentalism is rightly oriented in its insistence on the divine inspiration of the Bible, inerrancy of the Word of God, and such biblical truths as the Five Fundamentals, it is nevertheless rooted in an ideology that is not biblical, despite the disclaimers of its proponents. For it insists on an unyielding adherence to rigid doctrinal attitudes and an unquestioning, uncritical reading of the Bible as the sole source of teaching about Christian life and salvation.

The basic problem of the fundamentalist reading of the Bible is its failure to reckon with the truth of the Incarnation itself, its flight from the interplay of the divine and the human in approaching God. It has difficulty in admitting that God's Word has been couched in *human* language and has been produced under divine inspiration by human authors with varied abilities and resources, gifted, limited, or otherwise. It tends to treat the biblical text as though it were dictated verbatim by the Spirit and fails to recognize that God's Word has been formulated in time-conditioned human language and phraseology. It neglects the literary genres and modes of human thought in which texts have been formulated over long periods of time in diverse historical situations. It also insists unduly on the inerrancy of details, especially those dealing with historical or would-be scientific matters, and tends to regard as historical everything narrated in the past tense without regard for what might have been intended only as symbolic or figurative. It can also be very narrow in its outlook, seeing reality in an antiquated biblical world-view that inhibits dialogue with a wider view of culture and belief. It often uses an uncritical reading of some biblical texts to derive from them political conceptions and social attitudes that are prejudiced, racist, and simply contrary to the Christian gospel itself. Finally, in its dependence on the principle of *sola Scriptura*, fundamentalism severs the interpretation of the Bible from the Spirit-guided tradition that genuinely grew out of it within the Christian faith-community. It is thus often anti-church, neglecting creeds, dogmas, and liturgical practices that are part of the ecclesiastical tradition.[7]

Catholic fondness for this sort of literal interpretation has manifested itself in recent times, often in covert ways. For instance, there are those who call for a return to a "precritical" mode of interpretation, or for a return to a theological interpretation of the Bible. For the Christian reader seeks "not a dead word, imprisoned in the past, but a living word, addressed immediately to the man of today who takes part in the celebration of the liturgy, a word which concerns him, because it is for him that it was uttered and remains uttered."[8] So some Catholic readers of the Bible seek to justify their simplistic reading of the Bible.

In this connection it might be good to quote a few lines that the Biblical Commission incorporated into its document of 1984, *Bible et christologie*:

> Indeed, many problems still remain obscure about the composition process of the sacred writings that finally

---

[7] See further R. E. Brown, "Biblical Fundamentalism: How Should Catholics Respond?" *St. Anthony's Messenger* 98/1 (June 1990) 11–15; "The Fundamentalist Challenge: Suggestions for a Catholic Response," *Catholic Update* 590 (May 1990) 1–4.

[8] L. Bouyer, "Liturgie et exégèse spirituelle," *Maison-Dieu* 7 (1946) 27–50, esp. 30. Many other systematic theologians could be listed here: H. de Lubac, Y. Congar, et al. One should note in particular H. U. von Balthasar, whose ranting against "modern exegesis" was notorious; see, e.g., "Exegese und Dogmatik," *IKZ* 5 (1976) 385–92. Cf. J. Guitton, *Silence sur l'essentiel* (Paris: Desclée, 1986).

emerged from their inspired authors. As a result, those who would dispense with the study of problems of this sort would be approaching Scripture only in a superficial way; wrongly judging that their way of reading Scripture is "theological," they would be setting off on a deceptive route. Solutions that are too easy can in no way provide the solid basis needed for studies in biblical theology, even when engaged in with full faith (1.3.3).[9]

The Commission had discussed eleven different approaches to Christology in modern times and pointed out the risks that each one might run. Then it added an overview of the biblical testimony to Jesus the Christ. Nowhere in the document does the Commission speak of the historical-critical method, but in its effort to present an overview of an "integral Christology" (the total testimony of the Bible to Christ Jesus), it insisted time after time on "the demands of biblical criticism" (e.g., 1.2.7.2), which it clearly distinguished from "critical hypotheses . . . always subject to revision" (1.2.10). In the instance quoted above, the Commission was alluding to the claims of those who maintain that they prefer to interpret Scripture not historically, but theologically, or as did the Fathers of the Church. It thus expressed a necessary caution about the naiveté of such a would-be theological approach.

And yet, more has to be said. Although one has to recognize that normally there is one literal sense to most passages of Scripture, and that that meaning has usually to be regarded as its spiritual sense, as the inspired meaning of the sacred text through which God's Word addresses us today, yet the

---

[9] See *Bible et christologie* (Paris: Editions du Cerf, 1984) 69. An English translation of it can be found in my book, *Scripture and Christology: A Statement of the Biblical Commission with a Commentary* (New York/Mahwah, NJ: Paulist, 1986), esp. 56–58.

modern study of language and linguistics and of philosophical hermeneutics has made us aware in new ways of a multivalence of human discourse (and consequently of human writing).

Just as secular poetry and other literary forms can often express things on different levels or with a double sense, so too does the Bible on occasion. In fact, when the Fourth Gospel depicts Jesus saying to the Jews, "Destroy this temple, and in three days I will raise it up" (2:19), the evangelist himself takes pains to note, "But he was speaking about the temple of his body" (2:21). This saying his disciples recalled and only understood after he had been raised from the dead: "They believed the Scripture and the word which Jesus had uttered" (2:22). Similarly, the Fourth Gospel portrays Caiaphas the high priest saying, "You know nothing, and you do not realize that it is better for you that one man should die instead of the people, so that the nation may not perish." The evangelist then adds, "He did not say this on his own, but since he was high priest for that year, he prophesied that Jesus was going to die for the nation, and not only for the nation, but also to gather into one the dispersed children of God" (John 11:49–52). In these instances both Jesus' and Caiaphas's words clearly have to be understood on more than one level, and the evangelist calls attention to a deeper meaning, a prophetic utterance expressing a truth that goes beyond the political calculation of the high priest's immediate vision or the disciples' comprehension.

In such cases one sees that the literal sense of biblical utterances can carry at times a dynamic dimension surpassing their face value. But to admit this is not to return to the theory of the multiple senses of Scripture that was in vogue in the middle ages.

In this regard, the canonical sense of Scripture also makes its contribution to a meaning that surpasses the literal meaning attained by the historical-critical method rightly used.[10] Just how one works with such forms of more than a literal meaning is the task of theology. But to admit this more-than-literal sense does *not* mean that one can find such multivalence of meaning *everywhere* in the Bible. On the contrary, it is of *highly limited* character. For as Paul the Apostle once said, "We write for you nothing but what you can read and understand" (2 Cor 1:13).[11] And to disregard that injunction about the literal meaning of Scripture would be to introduce all sorts of subjective eisegesis.

II. *The Spiritual Sense of Scripture*

The problem with the "spiritual sense" of Scripture is that it is not always used in a univocal way and has become a

---

[10] For instance, the Canticle of Canticles, so expressive of mutual human love between man and woman, was quickly understood in Judaism as an expression of the relationship of Israel and God. Indeed, this was the reason why it found its way into the Jewish canon, both Palestinian and Alexandrian. Yet when the Christian canon adopted that part of the Hebrew Scriptures, Canticles took on still another canonical sense, which led in time to multiple allegorical interpretations of it as expressive of the relation between the Church and Christ as the loved ones. See further R. E. Murphy, "Recent Literature on the Canticle of Canticles," *CBQ* 16 (1954) 1–11; "Patristic and Medieval Exegesis—Help or Hindrance?" *CBQ* 43 (1981) 505–16.

To take yet another example, the meaning of the Woman of Revelation 12, clothed with the sun, with the moon under her feet, and crowned with stars. The primary meaning of the woman is usually understood to be Israel giving birth to the Messiah and to other offspring, the Christian people of God, the Church. So one would have to understand chap. 12, when the Book of Revelation is considered *in and for itself*. When that book is considered as part of the Christian canon, however, along with other New Testament writings, especially with the Gospels according to Luke and John, the various images of the Virgin, the woman at the foot of the cross, and the woman who gave birth to him who is for Christians "the Messiah," all conspire to yield what may be a canonical sense, which was further allegorized in the mariological interpretation of this chapter that came to the fore in the fourth century. See further R. E. Brown et al., *Mary in the New Testament: A Collaborative Assessment by Protestant and Roman Catholic Scholars* (Philadelphia, PA: Fortress; New York/Ramsey, NJ: Paulist, 1978) 219–39.

[11] See G. Martin, *Reading Scripture as the Word of God* (Ann Arbor, MI: Word of Life, 1975) 32–37.

sort of weasel word. Hence one has to sort out the different meanings of the spiritual sense of Scripture.

First of all, when Pius XII spoke of the literal sense of Scripture (*Divino afflante Spiritu* §23), he related it clearly to the "theological doctrine in faith and morals of the individual books or texts" (§24). He realized, moreover, that the meaning of Scripture "clearly intended by God" could not be something other than "the literal meaning of the words, intended and expressed by the sacred writer" (§26). Yet he insisted that the Catholic interpreter had to "disclose and expound *this spiritual significance, intended and ordained by God*" (§27 [my italics]). This is why one must insist that the properly-oriented use of the historical-critical method brings to light within the Church or the community of faith *the literal sense precisely as the spiritual sense of the Word of God.*[12] In reality, the spiritual sense of Scripture is nothing other than the literal sense intended by the inspired human author.

The exposition of Scripture that seeks to set forth the meaning of the Word of God in this way would reduce to silence those who claim that "they scarcely ever find anything in biblical commentaries to raise their hearts to God, to nourish their souls or promote their interior life." This complaint about sterile commentaries comes from Pius XII himself in

---

[12] In the special paragraph devoted to the interpretation of Scripture in the dogmatic constitution on Divine Revelation, Vatican II, without ever mentioning the literal sense, set as the goal of the interpreter the investigation of "what the sacred writers really intended to convey and what God wanted to manifest by means of their words" (*Dei verbum* §12). Nor did it mention the spiritual sense, but it did maintain that "since Sacred Scripture must be read and interpreted according to the same Spirit by which it was written, no less serious attention must be given to the content and unity of the whole of Scripture, if the meaning of the sacred texts is to be brought to light, taking into account the living Tradition of the whole Church and the analogy of faith" (ibid.). In this last sentence the Council properly related the literal sense to its canonical setting and to the Tradition that grows out of it.

his encyclical (§25), and he may well have been referring to the writings of some commentators who have used the historical-critical method.[13] Yet the real question is, How have such commentators used that method? Do they allow presuppositions of faith to enhance and enrich its own proper effects? Do they seek to elucidate this literal, spiritual sense? If I have insisted on an identification of the literal sense of Scripture with the spiritual sense, it is because of what Pius XII said about the former and because of the legitimacy of such an identification today.

Moreover, this identification explains how Jewish readers in the twentieth century would still find in the Hebrew Scriptures the spiritual sense of the Word of God intended for them, which nourishes their interior lives, and even how Christians readers can find in the literal sense of Old Testament writings food for their spiritual lives too.

But the "spiritual sense" of Scripture has not always been so understood, and this leads to the other ways in which it has been employed.

Second, following a traditional, patristic usage, Pius XII himself employed the term to mean that what was said and done in the Old Testament "prefigured in a spiritual way" what was to come in the new dispensation of grace (§26). In other words, he used the term to mean the reading of the Old Testament in a christological sense. In this way, canonical criticism helps to explain the added sense that Christian readers find in the Old Testament as related to the New. This was what Augustine meant when he wrote, *In Vetere Novum (Testamentum) latet, et in Novo Vetus patet*, in the Old the New [Testament] lies hidden, and in the New the Old is unfolded.

---

[13] Pius XII cited no examples so that one can only guess that he had in mind some commentators who have used this method.

This would make the "spiritual" understanding of the Old Testament different for Christians from that of their Jewish brothers and sisters. This Christian understanding of the Old Testament thus constitutes, in reality, an *added* spiritual sense, a christological spiritual sense of Old Testament books. It is important to note that this was the sense in which Pius XII used that term in his encyclical, for it is a sense restricted to the Old Testament. In effect, Pius XII was adopting a venerable patristic usage.

For this "spiritual sense" of Scripture was developed by various patristic writers in their attempts to answer those who criticized Christian teachings, in their controversies with Jewish teachers, and especially in their way of reading the Old Testament in light of the Christ-event. They built upon the distinction of the Apostle Paul who claimed that God had made him a competent "minister of the new covenant, not of the letter, but of the spirit" (2 Cor 3:6). For many patristic writers, however, apart from those of the Antiochene school, this meant that they could freely take phrases from the Bible and, in ignoring their contextual sense, use them in a generic way to propound (Christian) truths revealed by God. This proved to be, indeed, a departure from the literal sense of the Bible, and such a global use of Scripture[14] resulted in allegorical and typological interpretations of the Old Testament to discover its "spiritual" meaning.

In this mainly christological way, the Bible as a whole was regarded as the Word of God transmitted to the Christian

---

[14] The global use of Scripture begins in Scripture itself. Luke depicts the risen Christ interpreting for the disciples on the way to Emmaus "every part of Scripture, beginning with Moses and all the prophets" and showing how "the Messiah was bound to suffer before entering his glory" (24:26–27). Yet one will look in vain for specific passages in the Old Testament that speak of a suffering Messiah, which is not the same as the suffering Servant of Deutero-Isaiah.

Church and was considered as being addressed thus to Christians even in their contemporary situation. Jesus Christ was considered the fulfillment of the Law and the Prophets, and key Old Testament texts viewed as messianic were applied to him, in imitation of the use of the Old Testament in many places in the New Testament itself.

Such a spiritual interpretation of Scripture can be found as early as the *Epistle of Barnabas*,[15] in the writings of Justin Martyr, especially in his *Dialogue with Trypho*, and in those of Tertullian. But the prime mover in this spiritual interpretation of the Old Testament was Origen, often considered "the first scientific exegete of the Catholic Church."[16] He distinguished three levels of Scripture: its body (what "simple" read-

---

[15] See, for example, the allegorical interpretation of the red heifer (of Numbers 19) in *Barn*. 8:1–7: "The calf is Jesus . . . and why was the wool put on the wood? Because the kingdom of Jesus is on the wood, and because those who hope in him will live forever. . . . For this reason the things that happened are plain to us, but obscure to them, because they did not listen to the voice of the Lord." Or the allegorical interpretation of the number 318, the men of his household that Abraham circumcised (by a conflation of Gen 17:23,27 and 14:14): "Learn richly then, beloved children, about all things, for Abraham, who first practised circumcision, looked forward in the spirit to Jesus and received the doctrines of three letters. For it says, 'Abraham circumcised the men of his household eighteen and three hundred.' What therefore was the knowledge granted him? Notice that it mentions the eighteen first, and after a pause it says three hundred. The eighteen are ι', 'ten' (and) η', 'eight.' (And there) you have Jesus. Because the cross was destined to be favored in the τ', it also mentions the three hundred. So it indicates Jesus in the two letters, and the cross in one. He knows this who made the gift of his teaching planted in us" (*Barn*. 9:7–9). At this early stage the allegorical interpretation was not yet called "spiritual."

[16] J. Quasten (*Patrology*, 2.45) says further: Origen's commentaries "are a strange mixture of philological, textual, historical, and etymological notes and theological and philosophical observations. The author's main interest is not the literal but the mystical sense, which he finds by applying the allegorical method" (p. 48). The term "spiritual sense" is traced to Origen: "For we are inclined to admit in regard to the whole of divine Scripture that it all has a spiritual sense (*to pneumatikon*), but not all of it has a bodily sense (*to sōmatikon*)" (*Peri Archōn* 4.3.5; GCS 22. 331; SC 268. 362). Cf. K. Rahner, "Le début d'une doctrine des cinq sens spirituels chez Origène," *RAM* 13 (1932) 113–45.

ers would find as its "common and immediate meaning"), its soul (what "a little more advanced" readers would "further" discover as its meaning), and its spirit (what the "perfect" or "spiritually mature" [1 Cor 2:6–7] readers would discern as "the shadow of the good things to come" [Heb 10:1]).[17] Sometimes Origen referred to the senses of Scripture as *historica, mystica,* and *moralis,*[18] and the relation of the moral to the historical or the mystical sense differed at times.[19] He maintained that the difficulties of the literal text were intended by God to spur the reader on to seek their spiritual meaning. In using both allegory and typology and in focusing his interpretation of the Old Testament christologically, he discovered meanings that went far beyond the literal sense. Origen was followed in such a spiritual interpretation of Scripture by Methodius, Didymus the Blind, and others.

Third, in the Middle Ages, as a heritage of the patristic period, the spiritual or mystical sense was not only distinguished from the literal but subdivided into three forms: the allegorical, the moral (or tropological), and the anagogic (or eschatological) senses. All four came to be summed up in the famous distich of the late thirteenth-century theologian Augustine of Dacia (actually of Denmark): *Littera gesta docet, quid credas allegoria, moralis quid agas, quid speres anagogia,* The letter teaches facts; allegory, what you are to believe; moral, what you are to do; and anagogic, what you are to hope for.

The patristic contribution to the interpretation of the Bible sought to treat it above all as the Word of God read and savored in the Christian community and its liturgy. That

---

[17] *Peri Archōn* 4.2.4; GCS 312–13. Cf. *Hom. in Numeros* 9.7; GCS 30. 63–64.

[18] *Hom. in Genesim* 2.6; GCS 39. 36; *Hom. in Exodum* 1.4; GCS 29. 149–50.

[19] See H. de Lubac, *Exégèse médiévale: Les quatre sens de l'Ecriture* (Théologie 41; 2 vols.; Paris: Aubier, 1959) 201–3.

emphasis was not only right, but such interpretation, consequently, had much to do with the formation of the Christian
canon, with the shaping of the dogmatic Tradition of the
Church in its basic christological and trinitarian orientations,
and with the developing liturgy. In these ways the patristic
interpretation was only bringing to the fore in an explicit fashion what was often only implicit or latent in Scripture.

Two examples of how this patristic interpretation rightly
functioned may be cited: the Trinity and Original Sin. The
historical-critical interpretation of the Bible would not find
the Trinity as such in the New Testament. It does discover,
indeed, the elements of the Trinity: a clear teaching about
God the Father, about Christ the Son, and about the holy
Spirit, as well as an inceptive teaching about the relations between them, especially in the Pauline letters and Johannine
writings. But it remained for patristic interpretation to unpack
the biblical term "God," to bring the elements into proper
focus, and to formulate in an unambiguous way the doctrine
of the Triune God and the relations between the three persons
of the Trinity. Thus, for instance, the patristic interpretation
resolved the ambiguity left by such Pauline statements as "the
Lord is the Spirit" (2 Cor 3:17), by understanding them in the
light of other passages such as "the grace of the Lord Jesus
Christ, the love of God, and the fellowship of the Holy Spirit"
(2 Cor 13:13), where the triad is enunciated.

In Rom 5:12–21 Paul teaches that Adam, in sinning,
affected all humanity in a causal way so that all human beings
share in his mortality and sinfulness. But it remained for Augustine to explain that causality in terms, not of imitation (as
Pelagius advocated), but of propagation or generation,[20] and

---

[20] See *De peccatorum meritis et remissione* 1.9.10; CSEL 60.12: "This is [said]
of propagation, not of imitation; for [if it were meant of imitation], he would have

thus the doctrine of *Peccatum originale*, Original Sin, came to formulation.[21]

Such patristic interpretation may well be regarded as the *sensus plenior* of New Testament passages, for within the dogmatic Tradition of the Church it has supplied in given cases the sense that God, the primary author of Scripture, intended over and above that envisaged by the human author. It may be regarded as the term of a trajectory, the starting-point of which can be found in the sacred writings themselves, in the human author's original literal sense of a given passage.[22] In such cases, the patristic sense, supplying the *sensus plenior* of biblical passages, has thus added to the literal sense of Scripture a sense important for the Christian Church and Christian theology. But not every passage in Scripture enjoys such a fuller sense; only those that are picked up in a later passage of Scripture or in the subsequent dogmatic Tradition of the Church are to be so recognized. There must be some control of this sort; otherwise Scripture itself would be open to widespread and subjective fuller senses.

When we look today at the patristic global use of Scrip-

---

said, 'Through the Devil.' " Cf. *Contra duas epistolas Pelagianorum* 4.4.7; CSEL 60. 527–28.

[21] Original sin is a term derived from Western Latin theology, *peccatum originale*. One will look in vain for an equivalent of *originale* in the Eastern Greek theological tradition. Greek theologians, to be sure, interpreted Paul's letter to the Romans and explained Adam's sin and its effects on humanity, but they did not speak of it as "original" sin. Of Eve, Theophilus of Antioch said that she was *archēgos hamartias*, "leader/pioneer of sin" (*Ad Autolycum* 2.28; PG 6. 1097; SC 20. 112). That is the same phrase that Cyril of Jerusalem uses of the Devil (*Catecheses* 2.4; PG 33. 385).

[22] More would have to be said about such a fuller sense, with which not everyone agrees. Cf. R. E. Brown, *The* Sensus Plenior *of Sacred Scripture* (Baltimore, MD: St. Mary's University, 1955); "The *Sensus Plenior* in the Last Ten Years," *CBQ* 15 (1963) 262–85; "The Problems of the 'Sensus Plenior,' " *ETL* 43 (1967) 460–69; "Hermeneutics," *NJBC* art. 71, §49–51.

ture, we recognize that it has often ridden roughshod over important distinctions in biblical theology, in failing to allow for the differences among legal, prophetic, and sapiential forms of Old Testament teaching or for Marcan, Matthean, Lucan, Johannine, and Pauline forms of New Testament teaching. Such distinctions in biblical theological teaching are not only important, but are necessary, being only an application of the difference of literary forms or genres in Scripture. Yet they were normally not part of the patristic way of interpreting Scripture.

When one hears today the call for a return to a patristic interpretation of Scripture, there is often latent in it a recollection of Church documents that spoke at times of the "unanimous consent of the Fathers" as the guide for biblical interpretation.[23] But just what this would entail is far from clear. For, as already mentioned, there were Church Fathers who did use a form of the historical-critical method, suited to their own day, and advocated a literal interpretation of Scripture, not the allegorical. But not all did so. Yet there was no uniform or monolithic patristic interpretation, either in the Greek Church of the East, Alexandrian or Antiochene, or in the Latin Church of the West. No one can ever tell us where such a "unanimous consent of the Fathers" is to be found, and Pius XII finally thought it pertinent to call attention to the fact that there are but few texts whose sense has been defined by the authority of the Church, "nor are those more numerous about which the teaching of the Holy Fathers is unanimous."[24]

---

[23] Thus the Council of Trent in its decree of 1546 on the Latin Vulgate and the mode of interpreting Scripture (*EB* 62; DS 1507) and in its profession of faith (*EB* 73; DS 1863): *iuxta unanimem consensum Patrum*. Vatican I (*Constitutio dogmatica "Dei Filius," De fide catholica*) repeated it (*EB* 78; DS 3007).

[24] *Divino afflante Spiritu* §47; DS 3831; *EB* 565; *RSS* 565.

Origen's allegorical exegesis did not go without opposition, even in the Eastern Greek Church, for though many in the Alexandrian school adopted it, the Antiochene school, founded by Lucian of Antioch, resisted it, along with Diodore of Tarsus, John Chrysostom, and Theodore of Mopsuestia. A major proponent of the literal sense, no less than Theodore, was in time accused of reverting to a Jewish understanding of the Old Testament. In the Western Church Jerome, who at times criticized the Origenist interpretation of the Old Testament, also proposed the spiritual sense of many Old Testament passages. The result was that by the end of the patristic period most interpreters of Scripture oscillated between the literal and the spiritual sense, depending on the issue that was being discussed. This resulted in the medieval fourfold sense of Scripture mentioned earlier.

To the resultant multiplicity of senses of Scripture Christians of a later date also reacted. No less a person than Thomas Aquinas, who, though he reckoned with the four senses in vogue in his day, maintained that "all the senses are based on one, namely the literal, from which alone an argument can be drawn, and not from those which are said by way of allegory. . . . Yet nothing is lost to sacred Scripture because of this, because nothing necessary for faith is contained in the spiritual sense, which Scripture does not clearly pass on elsewhere by the literal sense."[25] Significantly, Aquinas understood the

---

[25] "Et ita etiam nulla confusio sequitur in sacra Scriptura: cum omnes sensus fundentur super unum, scilicet litteralem; ex quo solo potest trahi argumentum, non autem ex his quae secundum allegoriam dicuntur, ut dicit Augustinus in epistola contra Vincentium Donatistam. Non tamen ex hoc aliquid deperit sacrae Scripturae: quia nihil sub spirituali sensu continetur fidei necessarium, quod Scriptura per litteralem sensum alicubi manifeste non tradit" (*Summa Theologiae* 1, q. 1, a. 10 ad 1). This idea of the other senses being based on the literal sense is reiterated by Pope Benedict XV, *Spiritus Paraclitus* (AAS 12 [1920] 385–422, esp. 410-11; *EB* §485–86).

literal sense to be that "quem auctor intendit," which the author intended.[26]

So it is not surprising that Pius XII also warned about senses other than the literal. He exhorted Catholic interpreters to "refrain scrupulously from proposing as the genuine meaning of Sacred Scripture other figurative senses" (§27). Although he conceded that a figurative sense may be needed in preaching, it was to be used sparingly: "it should never be forgotten that this use of the Sacred Scripture is, as it were, extrinsic to it and accidental, and that, especially in these days, it is not free from danger" (§27).

These different senses of Scripture have influenced the relation of Scripture and Tradition, which together as a unit pass on to us the Word of God, the object of theological inquiry and study.

III. *Scripture as Related to Theology within the Church*

The coinherence of Scripture and Tradition or *Scripture interpreted* is the primary object of theological study. Indeed, if Scripture is to function as the "soul of sacred Theology," then one has to reckon with Scripture in its own formulation and its own theology. To put this another way, Scripture has to exercise a normative role, indeed, *the* normative role, in theology as well as in the life of the Church.[27]

This authoritative character of Scripture is reckoned with as early as Ben Sira, who in his Greek prologue refers to important truths handed down "through the law, the prophets, and those who followed them." Here we have the earliest ref-

---

[26] *S. T.* 1, q. 1, a. 10 resp. dic. (ad finem).

[27] See D. Hattrup, "Exegese und Theologie: Eine dogmatische Anmerkung," *TGl* 83 (1993) 90–94. Cf. J. Ernst and A. Lindemann, *TGl* 82 (1992) 457–69; R. E. Brown, "Scripture and Dogma Today," *America* 157/12 (31 October 1987) 286–89.

erence to what may have been an awareness of a canon of Scripture, of a collection of normative and authoritative sacred writings. Similarly, at the end of the Lucan Gospel the risen Christ refers to "the law of Moses, the prophets, and the psalms" (24:44) as containing authoritative teaching about him. But these are rare references, indeed, within the Bible to the idea of authoritative "Scripture." In the Greek form of Old Testament we find on a few occasions the use of *hē graphē* in the sense of "Scripture." Thus in 1 Chr 15:15, whereas the Hebrew Masoretic Text says, "as Moses had ordained according to the word of the Lord," the Greek of the Septuagint renders it, "as Moses had ordained in the word of God according to Scripture" (*kata tēn graphēn*). Cf. 2 Chr 30:5;[28] 30:18.

When one looks in Scripture itself for the idea of Tradition, there is again little to be mentioned. In the New Testament both the noun *paradosis*, "tradition," and the verb *paradidonai*, "to hand on" (a teaching), are found. Yet neither of these usages appears in the Greek Old Testament, save in some deuterocanonical books.[29] In the later rabbinical writings *paradidonai* is expressed as *māsar*; yet this Hebrew verb occurs but rarely in the Masoretic Text of the Bible, and then only in the sense of "handing over, delivering up" persons (Num 31:5,16). But in deuterocanonical Wis 14:15 the author tells of a father who fashioned an image of his dead son "and handed on to his subjects mysteries and rites."[30]

Thus the Old Testament itself is not a real source for any

---

[28] Here *kata tēn graphēn* renders Hebrew *kakkātûb*, "as was written."

[29] Even Y. M.-J. Congar in his classic treatment, *Tradition and Traditions: An Historical and Theological Essay* (New York: Macmillan, 1966), could cite in his first chapter ("The Existence of Tradition in the Old and New Testament") scarcely anything from the Old Testament that is relevant beyond what has been mentioned above.

[30] This sense of *paradidonai* is also found in extrabiblical Greek writers: Plato, *Philebus* 16c ("those of old . . . passed on this report"). Cf. Diodorus Siculus, 5.48.4.

biblical teaching about normative tradition or for the idea of
a relation between Scripture and Tradition. And yet, in the
Old Testament writings one has to reckon with the prehistory
of some books. For instance, the documentary hypothesis and
its analysis of the Pentateuch reveal that a normative tradition
antedated the final redaction of the Pentateuch. Whether oral
or written, such sources were utilized by the authors and redacted by them to their literary and religious purposes in what
became eventually the written Word of God. The oracles of
the prophet Jeremiah exerted no little influence on Ezekiel,
Daniel, certain psalms, and Deutero-Isaiah, but in what form
this influence was felt is hard to say. The compilation and redaction of Jeremiah's oracles in writing was probably the work
of his assistant Baruch after the prophet's death. Such isolated
traces of oracular tradition regarded as normative can thus be
detected in the Old Testament, but they are not numerous.

In the New Testament, where the words and deeds of
Jesus of Nazareth are recorded, we detect an awareness of
"tradition" related to Scripture. In Mark 7, in a dispute with
some Pharisees and Scribes, Jesus is asked why his disciples
do not follow "the tradition of the elders" (v. 3), i.e., about
washing their hands before eating. Jesus rejoins by calling it
"a human tradition," which he sets over against "God's commandment." He accuses them of "nullifying God's word in
favor of traditions you have handed on" (Mark 7:9–13; cf.
Matt 15:21–28). Here a special contrast is made between human tradition and "the Word of God," i.e., Scripture, referring to the Fourth Commandment (Exod 20:12). The idea of
a tradition as normative is present here, even if Jesus rejects

---

See E. Pfister, *Philologus* 69 (1915) 415. In most of these instances it is a question of
oral tradition.

the Pharisaic notion of it.[31] Thus a gospel episode warns Christians about the negative role that tradition, when its origin is human, can play. In effect, it denies a normative role to such human tradition and severs all connection of it with Scripture. Yet apart from this isolated episode there is no other saying of Jesus that would bear on the relation of Tradition to Scripture.

However, in other parts of the New Testament one finds traces of such a relationship. On the one hand, Paul refers to the Old Testament Scriptures as *graphai hagiai*, "holy Scriptures" (Rom 1:2), thus recognizing their authority. He maintains, however, that these writings were not composed solely for the people of old. Having quoted Gen 15:6 about the justification of Abraham because of his faith, he says that those words were not written for Abraham's sake alone, but for ours too (Rom 4:24; cf. 15:4). He thus modernizes the sense of an Old Testament passage and actualizes its pertinence.

On the other hand, Paul is also aware of a Tradition within the early church to which he is tributary and which he regards as normative. "For I have received from the Lord, what I also passed on to you" (1 Cor 11:23). So he introduces his account of the Last Supper. Here he uses the official words of Tradition: *parelabon*, "I received," and *paredōka*, "I passed on."[32] A still more instructive passage is 1 Corinthians 15, where Paul adapts part of the early kerygma:

---

[31] Josephus also mentions such traditions: "The Pharisees passed on to the people certain regulations transmitted by former generations, which are not recorded in the laws of Moses" (*nomima tina paredosan . . . ek paterōn didochēs, haper ouk anagegraptai en tois Mōyseōs nomois, Ant.* 13.10.6 §297). Cf. *Ant.* 10.4.1 §51; 13.16.2 §408 (*kata tēn patrōan paradosin*). Cf. Philo, *De spec. leg.* 4.28 §150.

[32] Even though we have already noted that these expressions have no role in the Greek Old Testament and have no Hebrew equivalents in the Masoretic Text, they reflect the standard vocabulary that will emerge in the later rabbinical writings:

I remind you, brethren, in what terms (*tíni logō*) I preached to you the gospel, which you received (*ho kai parelabete*) and in which you stand firm; through it you will also be saved, if you hold fast to it. For I handed on to you (*paredōka hymin*) as of first importance what I also received (*parelabon*), that Christ died for our sins according to the Scriptures, that he was buried, that he was raised on the third day according to the Scriptures, and that he appeared . . . (15:1–5).

So Paul cites the primitive kerygma of the church that existed before him in relation to his own preaching of the gospel, and he cites it as a normative Tradition. Cf. 1 Cor 11:2.

Such biblical data about the relation of Scripture and Tradition are not numerous. Yet what there is instructs us that both Scripture and Tradition were regarded as normative for the teaching of the primitive Christian community. Early Christians regarded Scripture, in the sense of the Old Testament, as normative: "All Scripture is inspired by God and useful for teaching, for reproof, for correction, and for training in righteousness, so that the one who belongs to God may be competent, equipped for every good work" (2 Tim 3:16–17). Although no similar statement can be found about Tradition, one New Testament writer at least did not hesitate to appeal to traditions that he had passed on as authoritative: "Stand firm, therefore, brethren, and hold fast to the traditions that you were taught by us whether by word of mouth or by a letter" (2 Thess 2:15).

It is often said that the New Testament is the Church's

---

qibbēl, "receive" (a teaching), and *māsar*, "hand on" (a teaching). Cf. B. Gerhardsson, *Memory and Manuscript: Oral Tradition and Written Transmission in Rabbinic Judaism and Early Christianity* (ASNU 22; Uppsala: Almqvist & Wiksells, 1961) 288–323.

book, meaning that a generation of the early Christian community existed and was governed by an oral Tradition that sprang from the words and deeds of Jesus of Nazareth before the Christian Scriptures, the New Testament, were composed. This is true, but one must also recall that the early Christian community, even after the death and resurrection of Jesus Christ, did have the Old Testament as the written Word of God in the strict sense along with its own oral traditions, part of which was only later consigned to writing. For these early Christians in pre-New Testament times Tradition did not exist alone; as it was being fashioned, it developed in consonance with the Hebrew Scriptures, with the written Word of God of old.

Moreover, that early Tradition did not continue to develop in isolation of the Christian Scriptures of the New Testament as they were coming into being. Today we have access to that early Christian Tradition only through the New Testament itself. Hence the insistence of modern theologians on the coinherence of Scripture and Tradition. As Vatican II put it, the two, Scripture and Tradition, "form one sacred deposit of the Word of God, which is committed to the Church" (*Dei verbum* §10).[33] As Card. J. Ratzinger has said in his commentary on this Council document, "It is stated that Scripture *is* the Word of God consigned to writing. Tradition, however, is described only functionally, in terms of what it *does*: it hands on the word of God, but *is* not the word of God."[34]

---

[33] Card. Ratzinger has described the situation thus: ". . . the relation should not be understood in terms of a mechanical juxtaposition, but as an organic interpenetration" or as "the indissoluble interpenetration of Scripture and tradition" (*Commentary on the Documents of Vatican II* [ed. H. Vorgrimler; 5 vols.; New York: Herder and Herder, 1967–69] 3. 191).

[34] Ibid., 194 (his emphasis). Elsewhere Card. Ratzinger is quoted as having said, "There is a mutual relationship here: The Bible interprets the church, and the church interprets the Bible. Again, this must be a mutual relationship. We cannot seek refuge

Tradition is regarded as a genuine norm since it is "a legitimate unfolding of biblical data."[35] Sometimes Tradition represents a process that may begin as a legitimate theological extension of a biblical teaching that is per se "open," i.e., which could develop in one way or another. Catholics see this development as Spirit-guided so that it becomes part of the Church's living faith and dogmatic Tradition.

By way of example in a negative sense, one may point, to the *open* character of John 13:12–15, where Jesus is depicted telling his disciples that they should wash one another's feet in imitation of his action at the Last Supper. That act could conceivably have developed in the Tradition into a sacrament, as a theological extension of the command expressed. But it did not so develop, despite the openness of the biblical instruction. Similarly, in a positive sense, the *open* character of the teaching in Jas 5:14 about elders of the church being summoned to anoint the sick with oil and to pray over them led in time to the Sacrament of the Anointing of the Sick. Such an extension of the meaning of a biblical verse is being called "theological," because it is per se not biblical. It is rather a conclusion drawn from a biblical text under the Spirit-guided development of Tradition.

However, some Catholic theologians believe that the idea of Scripture and Tradition forming "one sacred deposit of the Word of God" does not preclude the view of Scripture as *norma normans non normata* and of Tradition as *norma normata* for the faith of the Church and for theology.[36] Scripture,

---

in an ecclesiastical positivism. Finally, the last word belongs to the church, but the church must give the last word to the Bible" (P. T. Stallsworth, "The Story of an Encounter," *Biblical Interpretation* (n. 37 in chap. 1), 118.

[35] K. Rahner, "Scripture and Theology," *Theological Investigations* 6 (Baltimore, MD: Helicon, 1969) 89–97, esp. p. 92.

[36] See K. Rahner, "Scripture and Theology," 93: "We may therefore state quite confidently that for theology, scripture is in practice the only material source of faith

especially that of the New Testament, was born indeed of a preexistent Christian Tradition, a Tradition, however, that was already normed in no small way by the already existing (Old Testament) Scriptures. Though the New Testament has enshrined in writing part of the Christian Tradition, it has done this under the charism of biblical inspiration, a movement of God's Spirit that the Christian Tradition has always regarded as privileged and distinct from the Spirit's assistance in guiding the Church in its ongoing teaching, i.e., in its dogmatic definitions, either conciliar or papal. Such inspiration is recognized as a charism gracing not only the New Testament, but the Old Testament as well. Thus the written Word of God has become a testimony without peer to guide the faith of the people of God. In saying this, I am not identifying Scripture with revelation or with the Word of God, pure and simple. Yet as the *written* Word of God it does stand over the dogmatic Tradition that springs from it and over the Church's magisterium that serves the Word of God, handing it on, guarding it scrupulously, and explaining it faithfully—all with the assistance of the Spirit.[37] For this reason in that complex of the one sacred deposit of the Word of God, Scripture may be regarded as the *norma normans non normata*, the norm that norms (but is) not normed, because it is unmanipulable (*unverfügbar*) by either the Tradition or the magisterium. "Therefore, like the Christian religion itself, all the preaching of the Church must

---

to which it has to turn as being the absolutely original, underived source and *norma non normata*." See also his article, "Bible. B. Theology," *Sacramentum mundi* (6 vols.; New York: Herder and Herder, 1968–70) 1. 171–78, esp. 176–77: "Even the magisterium which interprets Scripture under the assistance of the Spirit does not thereby place itself above Scripture but under it (cf. *Dei Verbum*, art. 10); it knows that Scripture brought into existence by the Spirit and read by the Church with the assistance of the Spirit conveys its true meaning. In that way Scripture remains the *norma non normata* of theology and the Church."

[37] *Dei verbum* §10.

be nourished and ruled by sacred Scripture."[38] Tradition, however, is the *norma normata* (the normed norm), i.e., it is normed by Scripture. Thus related to Tradition, Scripture is the source of the life of faith in the Christian community, and hence the wellspring of theology.

What about teachings that emerge in the Tradition that are not contained in Scripture as such? Here the Catholic view has espoused the principle enunciated long ago by Augustine: *Non quia Scriptura dicit, sed quia Scriptura non contradicit,* Not because Scripture says it, but because Scripture does not contradict it.[39] In this regard I again recall the idea of the openness of Scripture, which may develop in a certain direction, and not in another. Such teachings are clearly part of the dogmatic theologian's bailiwick and task.

The relationship between Scripture and Tradition is one that intimately affects the study of theology. For the theologian is always confronted with the problem of how one is to regard the seminal teachings of Scripture and allow for the flowering of such teaching as it develops into full-blown forms. The acorn is not an oak; but there is no oak without an acorn. The organic unity between the two is essential. Suppose Scripture does not contain an example, a promise, or a command as the basis of a certain teaching, is that teaching absolutely excluded, even if it can be seen only as a development or a theological extension of some seminal biblical doctrine?[40]

Furthermore, in this regard one has to draw a distinction

---

[38] *Dei verbum* §21.

[39] *De Trin.* 7.4.8; CCLat 50. 258; PL 42.941.

[40] It is important also to recall the view of Cyprian: *Traditio sine veritate vetustas erroris*, Tradition without truth is but error grown old (*Ep.* 74.9). This view of Cyprian is important because it cautions against what may be only human tradition in the Church and in theology. In this regard, one would have to insist again on the Spirit-guided character of the Tradition that develops. The assistance of the Spirit is what preserves the Tradition from error and guarantees it in the truth.

between biblical theology and systematic theology. Years ago, Krister Stendahl wrote an influential article on these topics.[41] He described the function of biblical theology as descriptive, whereas that of systematic theology was normative. For him, biblical theology tells us what the Bible meant, whereas systematic theology tells us what it means today. His view has often been debated.[42] In my estimation, he drew a dichotomy between the two that is not entirely acceptable. For biblical theology is not only descriptive. It too is normative, albeit in an inceptive way. In other words, for a Christian in the twentieth century the synthesis of the teaching of a New Testament writer, say Paul or John, is not only descriptive, but is also normative. I, as a Christian, have to believe that Christ Jesus has justified me, saved me, reconciled me to the Father, etc., as Paul has described effects of the Christ-event.[43] And I, as a Christian, have to believe that I, a branch, shall bear fruit (= live a holy life) only if I remain in union with Christ, the vine. The study of Pauline theology synthesizes the Apostle's teaching on justification, salvation, and reconciliation, indeed, not just to achieve a description of them, but precisely as a synthesis of such normative and important doctrines. It is an inceptive norm, however, because biblical theology in itself is not the whole story, and that is where Tradition and systematic theology enter in to interpret the inceptive teaching. Systematic theologians of today cannot spin off the top of their heads an explanation of justification wholly severed of its biblical roots; it is rather their job to reformulate, perhaps even to

---

[41] "Biblical Theology, Contemporary," *IDB* 1. 418–32.

[42] See, for example, A. Dulles, "Response to Krister Stendahl's 'Method in the Study of Biblical Theology,' " *The Bible in Modern Scholarship* (ed. J. P. Hyatt; Nashville, TN: Abingdon, 1965) 210–16.

[43] See further my *Paul and His Theology: A Brief Sketch* (Englewood Cliffs, NJ: Prentice Hall, 1989) 59–71.

reconceptualize, the inceptive biblical teaching on such a topic in the light of Tradition and new developments in the life of the Church. In this way biblical theology is a prime and normative factor in the study of the Sacred Page, which is the "soul of sacred Theology."

The relation of Scripture to theology may be viewed from still another viewpoint. Years ago K. Rahner wrote an article, "Exegese und Dogmatik," in which he discussed the relation between them. It was actually more of a discussion of the roles of the exegete and the dogmatic theologian, and in the original German he used a device that is lost in English translation. When he addressed the exegetes, he employed the formal form *Ihr*, "You," but when he spoke to dogmatic theologians, he addressed them familiarly with *Du*, "Thou," thus classing himself with his systematic peers.[44] In the article Rahner complained about the tactics of both exegetes and dogmaticians. To the exegetes he said: You must remember that you too "are Catholic theologians," that you must pay attention to "the Catholic principles governing the relationship between exegesis and dogmatic theology," that you must learn to build a bridge from your investigations and interpretations to the rest of theology, and that you should have "a more exact knowledge of scholastic theology."[45] But he also chided his colleagues in systematic theology:

> You know less about exegesis than you should. As a dogmatic theologian you rightly claim to be allowed to engage

---

[44] "Exegese und Dogmatik," *Stimmen der Zeit* 168 (1961) 241–62; repr. in *Schriften zur Theologie* (16 vols.; Einsiedeln: Benziger, 1954–84) 5 (1964) 82–111. The article can be found in English, "Exegesis and Dogmatic Theology," *Theological Investigations* (21 vols.; Baltimore, MD: Helicon; New York: Crossroad, 1961–88) 5 (1966) 67–93.

[45] Ibid., 70–74.

in the work of exegesis and biblical theology in your own right, and not just to accept the results of the exegetical work of the specialist. For it is your job as a dogmatic theologian to use all available means for listening to the word of God wherever it is pronounced—and where better than in Holy Scripture? But then you must perform the work of exegesis in the way it has to be done today and not in the way you used to do it in the good old days—or better, not only in the old way. Your exegesis in dogmatic theology must be convincing also to the specialist in exegesis.[46]

Rahner acknowledged that "the exegete has the right and the duty to do the work of the historian of fundamental theology in connection with the New Testament, precisely if and because he should be a Catholic theologian who may not simply start from the bare and unproved act of faith. Hence, he does not always need to begin by simply presupposing the inspiration and inerrancy of Scripture in every case."[47]

Rahner first penned those words in 1961, and much has happened since.[48] Though he himself was not a good example

---

[46] Ibid., 77. "Exegese und Dogmatik," 93. The full quotation runs thus: "Lieber Freund, sei ehrlich: Du verstehst von Exegese weniger, als wünschenswert wäre. Du machst als Dogmatiker mit Recht den Anspruch, eigenen Rechtes Exegese und biblische Theologie treiben dürfen und nicht bloss die Ergebnisse der Fachexegeten zu benehmen, weil es deine Aufgabe als Dogmatiker selbst ist, mit allen Mitteln auf das Wort Gottes zu hören, wo immer es ergeht, und es nirgends besser gefunden werden kann als in der Heiligen Schrift. Aber dann musst du Exegese treiben, wie man es heute tun muss, nicht wie man dies in den guten alten Zeiten getan hat. Oder besser: nicht nur so. Deine Exegese in der Dogmatik muss auch für den Fachexegeten bezeugend sein."

[47] "Exegesis," 78–79.

[48] For an instance of the way a Catholic exegete has responded to the kind of criticism that Rahner expressed, see R. E. Brown, "Scripture and Dogma Today," *America* 157/12 (31 October 1987) 286–89; also his *Biblical Exegesis and Church Doctrine* (New York/Mahwah, NJ: Paulist, 1985); "Historical-Critical Exegesis and Attempts at Revisionism," *The Bible Today* 23/3 (1985) 157–65.

of a dogmatic theologian who engaged in exegesis as it should be practised,[49] there have been better examples since then, e.g., E. Schillebeeckx or W. Kasper.[50]

Yet all have not heeded Rahner's advice. To cite one recent example. In *Theological Studies* for 1992 there is an article on "The Faith of Jesus," written by G. O'Collins and D. Kendall.[51] It begins with an important section on "the nature of faith," drawing the distinction that is crucial to the discussion between *fides quae*, the content of what Jesus believed, and *fides qua*, the personal commitment involved in such faith. It goes on to treat Jesus' human knowledge especially in light of the debate inherited from Thomas Aquinas and reflected in more recent Church documents, *Lamentabili*, a decree of the Holy Office in 1918, the encyclical *Mystici Corporis*, and three pronouncements of the International Theological Commission on Christology.[52] All of these texts reveal a remarkable change of position that no longer insists that Jesus during his earthly

---

[49] Note his remark in *Foundations of Christian Faith: An Introduction to the Idea of Christianity* (Crossroad Book; New York: Seabury, 1978) 14: "In reflecting . . . upon the historical credibility of the resurrection and upon the self-understanding of Jesus that is ascribed to him by dogmatic theology, we can make use of only as much scriptural data here as is sufficiently certain today from an honest exegesis. By the very nature of the foundational course, as distinguished from *later and necessary* biblical theology, fundamental theology, ecclesiology and dogmatic theology, we may include only as much exegesis and biblical theology in the foundational course as is absolutely necessary. Then later exegesis and biblical theology can gather, organize and incorporate the rest of the positive, biblical material which must also be included in the church's theology." One senses here a begrudging attitude toward Scripture: unfortunately one has to deal with it, willy nilly.

[50] In saying this, I do not necessarily approve of all their exegesis, especially that of Schillebeeckx, who has depended too much on German Protestant interpreters, when he should have been reading more moderate contributions of their Catholic peers.

[51] *TS* 53 (1992) 403–23.

[52] See DS 3434, 3645–47, 3812; M. Sharkey, *International Theological Commission: Texts and Documents 1969–1985* (San Francisco, CA: Ignatius, 1989) 185–205, 197–223, 305–16.

life enjoyed the beatific vision. From their survey O'Collins and Kendall conclude only that Jesus was "(humanly) conscious of (1) his divine identity as Son of God and (2) his revealing/redemptive mission."[53] Then they take up the question of Jesus' human faith as it appears in Scripture, both outside the Gospels and in the Synoptics. There is little problem with the way they discuss Rev 14:12 ("faith of Jesus") and eight passages in the Pauline corpus ("the faith of Jesus Christ," Rom 3:22, 26; Gal 2:16a, 16b, 20; 3:22; Eph 3:12; Phil 3:9), as interpreted by various recent commentators. They find that growing numbers of interpreters admit that faith was an operative factor in the life of the earthly Jesus, who was himself "a model and exemplar of faith." Then they turn to a number of sayings of Jesus recorded in the Synoptic Gospels, seeking to derive from them what could have been the content of Jesus' faith during his earthly life and ministry. Finally, they conclude that what Jesus believed (his *fides quae*)

> did not coincide perfectly with that of later Christians. In some ways it was different even from the faith of his Jewish contemporaries, inasmuch as, for example, he knew and could not in the technical sense of the word confess the existence of God. At the same time, Jesus' confession of faith could coincide substantially with that of contemporary and earlier Jews. An analogous approach to the content of faith allows for similarities and differences between the faith of devout Jews, Jesus' faith, and subsequent Christian faith.[54]

Although the discussion of O'Collins and Kendall makes some good points about the faith of Jesus, its treatment of the

---

[53] *TS* 53 (1992) 411.
[54] Ibid., 421.

biblical data is faulted. They fail to make clear the distinction between what New Testament writers outside the Gospels attribute to Jesus in what they call his "faith" and what the Gospels may portray as his psychological awareness. Moreover, they cite D. Tracy's comment that the "psychology of Jesus is unavailable to modern scholarship,"[55] only to dismiss it and thus fail to perceive its pertinence to their discussion. Further, they fail to reckon with the complexity of the Synoptic problem, and this weakens their entire approach. If, indeed, "the Synoptic Gospels do not aim at presenting the inner life of Jesus, and as documents written out of faith, they cannot be read as 'normal' historical sources," do they, then, really permit us in "the authentic sayings they preserve" to "reach some modest, yet important conclusions about his interior dispositions"?[56] In the failure to reckon with the three stages of the gospel tradition, which are clearly related to this question and which have been part of the Catholic biblical interpreter's method at least since the Instruction of the Biblical Commission in 1964, their article turns out to be a good example of exegesis as it was done "in the good old days." Can one really psychoanalyze Jesus himself on the basis of documents compiled a generation at least after the facts that they describe, even if they do preserve in some fashion "authentic sayings"?

More important is the relation between Scripture and theology implied in the O'Collins-Kendall approach, which glosses over an important aspect. For the faith of Christians in the twentieth century is not based solely on what exegetes or theologians can reconstruct as the inner dispositions of Jesus of Nazareth or even on the gospel that he preached as recon-

---

[55] *The Analogical Imagination* (New York: Crossroad, 1981) 326.
[56] *TS* 53 (1992) 415–16.

structed by historical research. It is rather normed by the figure of Jesus of Nazareth as passed on to us by the early Christian Church in that Tradition that is enshrined in the Scriptures.[57] The two have to be kept in tandem: Jesus of Nazareth as the definitive revealer of God his Father *and* the early testimony to him in the Christian kerygma and its Scripture. These two, in tandem, supply the vitality both for Christian faith and Christian theology. For, as A. Dulles has put it, "The deeds of God in salvation history are not Christian revelation except as taken up into the preaching and memory of the Church, which treasures Scripture as a privileged text."[58] So whether the Jesus of history had "faith" and in what sense he may have had it is really of little importance for the faith of Christians in the twentieth century. That he may have been "a model and exemplar of faith" in the sense of his dedication and obedience to his Father is indeed part of the biblical (New Testament) teaching, as O'Collins and Kendall have well presented it. But that is the question of Jesus' *fides qua*, whereas the analysis of Jesus' *fides quae* as a factor for the faith of Christians today is relatively unimportant. Indeed, the meagre results of their investigation reveal its futility.

A similar difficulty can be found in what H. Küng has written about dogma versus the Bible or, as he paraphrases it, "Historico-Critical Exegesis as a Challenge to Dogmatic Theology."[59] Küng sees dogmatic theology separated by a gulf from historical-critical interpretation of the Bible. Whereas exegesis should be

---

[57] And not just in the New Testament, but in the total biblical testimony to him. See above p. 60.

[58] *The Craft of Theology: From Symbol to System* (New York: Crossroad, 1992) 81.

[59] *Theology for the Third Millennium: An Ecumenical View* (New York: Doubleday, 1988) 85–99.

the "basic theological discipline,"[60] it should open up "the way to the Jesus of history." Hence for Küng

> the order of the *original* (authentic) tradition of Jesus the Christ (*norma normans*), laid down in the New Testament, as opposed to all *subsequent* church tradition (*norma normata*), must have consequences for defining the relationship between exegesis and dogmatics.[61]

But Küng's call for a "historico-critically responsible dogmatic theology" is undermined by his identification of the *norma normans* with "the Jesus of history" alone. What Küng means by the Jesus of history is in reality "the historical Jesus," i.e., Jesus as reconstructed by historical research. This historical Jesus is not the same as the Jesus of history, the one who walked the roads of Palestine centuries ago and who evangelized the people of his time. He remains inaccessible to us; what little is known about him is that recovered by historical research, based mostly on a critical reading of the Gospels.[62] That reading properly results in "the historical Jesus," and his story cannot be reconstructed with unanimous consent, because it depends on the multiplicity of investigators; the most one can hope to attain is a generic agreement from such investigation.[63] But this "historical Jesus" is a human reconstruction. As such, it can never function as the *norma*

---

[60] This phrase Küng borrows from a Catholic New Testament interpreter, Josef Blank, "Exegesis als theologische Basiswissenschaft," *TQ* 159 (1979) 2–23.

[61] *Theology*, 86.

[62] The extrabiblical historical record about Jesus of Nazareth is meagre, indeed, being limited to a few testimonies that tell us very little about him; see my booklet, *A Christological Catechism: New Testament Answers* (rev. ed.; New York/Mahwah, NJ: Paulist, 1991) 11–14. Cf. J. P. Meier, *A Marginal Jew: Rethinking the Historical Jesus* (Anchor Bible Reference Library; New York: Doubleday, 1991) 56–111.

[63] For my attempt to present it briefly, see *A Christological Catechism*, 16–18.

normans of Christian faith or of theology.[64] It is no substitute for the written Word of God itself, for the inspired New Testament. If it were such a substitute, Scripture would cease to be the soul of theology.

Moreover, Küng in his insistence on "the Jesus of history" or "the *original* (authentic) tradition of Jesus" writes as a typical systematic theologian in his neglect of the Old Testament, which as part of the written Word of God is also part of the *norma normans* of Christian theology.[65] What is at fault here is the failure to recognize that two things have to be preserved in tandem, Jesus of Nazareth and the testimony to him that the Scriptures present. The latter is what the Biblical Commission called an "integral Christology," one that has listened to the whole of the biblical tradition, the Old Testament as well as the New Testament, since in the Christian view it all bears witness to Christ and has been given to us as the norm of Christian faith and theology.[66] Küng is right, however, when he castigates his dogmatic colleagues for sometimes blocking or ignoring "the findings of historico-critical exegesis (the Neo-Scholastic phase)" or sometimes going around them, disguising and domesticating them "(the phase of speculative harmonization)."[67] In this he is simply echoing, in effect, what K. Rahner said earlier, and when that happens, Scripture ceases to be the soul of sacred Theology.

I may conclude this discussion of the relation of Scripture

---

[64] This is likewise what is at fault in the feminist approach of E. Schüssler Fiorenza, *In Memory of Her* (New York: Crossroad, 1983).

[65] To be fair to Küng, I have to add that he eventually recognizes that the findings of exegesis have to be subjected to a systematic review "against the background of the history of dogma, theology, the Church, and the world" (pp. 86–87). The overall thrust of his discussion, however, tends to play this down.

[66] See *Scripture and Christology* (n. 9 above), 32 (§1.3.3), 92.

[67] *Theology*, 87.

to theology by quoting and commenting on a paragraph recently penned by A. Dulles. It runs:

> My own present leaning would be toward a method that
> makes use of historical-critical studies to assure a solid
> foundation in the biblical sources themselves, but does so
> under the continuous guidance of tradition and magiste-
> rial teaching. An adequate theological use of Scripture, I
> believe, would build also on the achievements of biblical
> theology and the kind of spiritual exegesis described
> above.[68] An interpretation that limited itself to the
> historical-critical phase would overlook the tacit mean-
> ings conveyed by the biblical stories, symbols, and meta-
> phors. A comprehensive approach, combining scientific
> and spiritual exegesis, does better justice to Catholic tra-
> dition and the directives of Vatican II, and better serves
> the needs of systematic theology.[69]

I agree with the use of the historical-critical method, as noted
here by Dulles, especially with his implied references to literary, rhetorical, and narrative refinements of the method.
Properly-oriented historical-critical exegesis, as already described, would also include biblical theology and the tacit
meanings of biblical stories, symbols, and metaphors. But one
would have to be on guard about the so-called spiritual exegesis, which Dulles would link with biblical theology and the
historical-critical method. He quotes the claims of some of its
modern proponents, who assert that what is important is the
realization that "Scripture . . . is *God speaking to man.* It

---

[68] Dulles refers here to his own description of "spiritual exegesis," as advocated
by L. Bouyer, H. de Lubac, H. U. von Balthasar, et al. See also R. Laurentin, *Comment reconcilier l'exégèse et la foi* (Paris: O. E. I. L., 1984); R. Guardini, "Heilige
Schrift und Glaubenswissenschaft," *Die Schildgenossen* 8 (1928) 24–57.

[69] *Craft of Theology* (n. 58 above), 85.

means a word that is not past but present, because eternal, a word spoken to me personally and not simply to others."[70] Interpreters who use the properly-oriented historical-critical method also maintain that Scripture is God speaking to human beings, eternally addressing them personally. But they would be reluctant to recognize as the Word of God much of the eisegetical fruits of the so-called spiritual interpretation of Scripture being advocated by some of the proponents of it cited by Dulles.[71]

I have been glad to address myself to this relation of Scripture and theology, which is that so frequently discussed by specialists in fundamental and dogmatic theology, by specialists who sit back and think and dream about how Scripture

---

[70] Quoted by Dulles from H. U. von Balthasar, "The Word, Scripture, and Tradition," in *Word and Revelation: Essays in Theology I* (New York: Herder and Herder, 1964) 9–30, esp. 26–27 (his italics). Von Balthasar also calls Scripture "the body of the logos" and denies that this patristic idea, according to which both the Eucharist and Scripture mediate to the faithful the one, incarnate logos, is "a merely arbitrary piece of allegorizing" (p. 15). But what else is it? This is a good example of the scholarly *Schwärmerei* to which those who advocate a spiritual exegesis of Scripture are led. It is not "exegesis" at all; it is *eisegesis*.

See also H. de Lubac, *The Sources of Revelation* (New York: Herder and Herder, 1968) 1–72, esp. 27–28: "The 'spiritual meaning' . . . is of necessity a view in faith. The meaning which stems from it is only perceived in the light of Christ and under the action of his Spirit, within his Church. One who takes up the study of the history of Israel's religion in this fashion gives all its historical importance to it, because he understands it as the salvation history of the Church. Strictly speaking, though, he does not study this salvation history as a historian, whose goal is to see the spectacle of events unfold before him; he meditates on it as a believer—in order to live by it. This is his own history, from which he cannot remove himself. This history interests him personally. It is a mystery which is also his own mystery, identically. Consequently, he does not question the Bible as he would any other document or series of documents about the past, but by the psychology of the Old Testament believers. Besides, he knows that they could not have been explicitly aware of everything which he discovers in their writings; the seals of the Book had to be broken by the Lion of the Tribe of Judah." It is great in theory, but how does it work out in practice? And how would a believing Jewish interpreter of the Old Testament understand that?

[71] E.g., L. Bouyer, H. U. von Balthasar, R. Guardini.

should be interpreted. They like to tell exegetes and biblical theologians how they should be doing their job, and yet they themselves have rarely, if ever, faced the difficult task of interpreting Scripture "in the way it has to be done today," as Rahner once put it. It is one thing to philosophize about the interpretation of Scripture, another thing to engage in it. It is easy to find fault with the historical-critical method of biblical interpretation, but such criticism lacks conviction, when the critics fail to show how the interpretation of Scripture should rather be carried out, other than invoking the use of an unspecified spiritual sense.[72]

---

[72] This is also what is problematic about the critique that Card. Ratzinger has written of modern biblical interpretation, and with that of H. U. von Balthasar. Both of them cite as an ideal model of interpretation Gregory of Nyssa's interpretation of the Canticle of Canticles (*Hom. in Canticum* 10 [ed. H. Langerbeck, 6. 295–296]; PG 44. 980). Cf. M. Canévet, *Grégoire de Nysse et l'herméneutique biblique: Etudes des rapports entre le langage et la connaissance de Dieu* (Paris: Etudes Augustiniennes, 1983). Yet how can that sort of interpretation be applied to other parts of the Old Testament (e.g., to the legal sections of the Pentateuch) or even to most of the New Testament? I fail to see how it can even be applied to the Book of Revelation, which has in its history been subject to much allegorical interpretation.

4. SCRIPTURE, THE BRIDGE IN ECUMENISM

Sacred Scripture not only plays an important role in the life of the Church and in Christian theology, but it has been in the course of this century an important bridge in the ecumenical dialogue between Christian Churches. In the history of Christianity the ecumenical movement is a phenomenon of the twentieth century during which Christians of various backgrounds, Orthodox, Protestant, and Roman Catholic, have sought not only to work together "so that the world may believe" (John 17:21), but also to surmount the historic divisions that have separated them from one another during the past millennium. Initially, that movement began among various Protestant denominations. In time, Orthodox churches joined it. After the Second World War and especially during the Second Vatican Council Roman Catholics became actively engaged in it. For the Council Fathers had recognized that Orthodox and Protestant Christians through faith in Christ and baptism have been "brought into a certain, though imperfect, communion with the Catholic Church"[1] and that such separated churches and communities "have by no means been deprived of significance and importance in the mystery of salvation."[2] The Council's Decree on Ecumenism acknowl-

---

[1] *Decree on Ecumenism* §3. See W. M. Abbott (ed.), *The Documents of Vatican II* (New York: Herder and Herder, and Association Press, 1066) 345.

[2] Ibid. (p. 346).

93

edged that "a love, veneration, and near cult of the sacred Scriptures lead our brethren to a constant and expert study of the sacred text. . . . Calling upon the Holy Spirit, they seek in these sacred Scriptures God as He speaks to them in Christ. . . ." Though the Council Fathers recognized that our separated brethren "think differently from us . . . about the relationship between the Scriptures and the Church . . . nevertheless, in dialogue itself, the sacred utterances are precious instruments in the mighty hand of God for attaining that unity which the Savior holds out to all."[3] Hence, the Catholic Church recognized officially the important role that Scripture has played in the ecumenical movement precisely because it is such a precious instrument in the hand of God in the struggle for Christian unity.

Although the ecumenical dialogues that have emerged since the Second Vatican Council between the Roman Catholic Church and various Protestant Churches have been the work of Catholic theologians mainly of systematic and historical disciplines, biblical interpreters have invariably been numbered among them. I personally have been involved in ecumenical dialogues in recent decades. At first I was a member of the Catholic team in dialogue with the Presbyterian and Reformed Churches in the United States. In 1967 I was appointed to the first phase of the Study Commission set up by the Vatican Secretariat for Promoting Christian Unity for dialogue on the international level with the Churches represented by the Lutheran World Federation. That phase of dialogue lasted for five years (1967–1971) and issued a pioneer document, the so-called Malta Report, a common statement in which we groped as we gradually learned to discuss together theological issues that had divided our Churches for over 400

---

[3] Ibid. §21 (pp. 362–63).

years.[4] In 1973 I was appointed to the national Lutheran-Catholic dialogue in the United States and have served as one of the biblical consultants until last year, when that dialogue reached a term in its relations. As a matter of fact, I replaced R. E. Brown, S.S., who had served as the biblical consultant on that dialogue since its inception in 1965. When I joined the national dialogue in 1973, it was just finishing its work on the fifth topic, Papal Primacy and the Universal Church. I was thus actively engaged in the dialogue rounds that debated Teaching Authority & Infallibility in the Church; Justification by Faith; the One Mediator, the Saints, and Mary; and the Word of God: Scripture and Tradition. I was also a member of the two task forces of American Catholic and Protestant biblical scholars who were assembled to discuss the topics, Peter in the New Testament and Mary in the New Testament. The results of that collaborative discussion were published as two books sponsored by the national Lutheran-Catholic dialogue, books that aided the dialogue in its work on the respective topics, even though they were not officially part of the dialogue proper. Moreover, from 1983 to 1988 I was also a member of the Catholic team that took part in the second phase of international dialogue between the Reformed Churches and the Catholic Church, which had been set up by the World Alliance of Reformed Churches and the Vatican Secretariate for Promoting Christian Union.

So I approach the question of Scripture as a bridge in ecumenism from this experience of over twenty-five years in

---

[4] The full report can be found in H. Meyer (ed.), *Evangelium—Welt—Kirche: Schlussbericht und Referate der römisch-katholisch / evangelisch-lutherischen Studienkommission "Das Evangelium und die Kirche", 1967–1971* (Frankfurt am M.: Lembeck/Knecht, 1975). The text of the common statement is given in both German (pp. 7–32) and English (pp. 33–58). The book also contains the position papers that were discussed. An English translation of the common statement can also be found in *Worship* 46 (1972) 326–51; *Lutheran World* 19 (1972) 259–73.

bilateral consultations with both Lutheran and Reformed-Church theologians. In discussing the topic, Scripture as a bridge in ecumenism, I shall order my remarks under three headings: (I) Scripture and Ecumenism; (II) Ecumenical translations of the Bible; and (III) Scripture in the Catholic-Lutheran Dialogue in the United States.

I. *Scripture and Ecumenism*

When one reflects on Scripture as the written Word of God and the role that it plays as the *norma normans non normata*[5] in the Church's life, teaching, worship, and theology, it becomes obvious that the Christian Church, in its present sadly divided forms, cannot ignore the influence that the written Word of God can provide for the modern ecumenical movement. Even if all the Churches engaged in this movement do not accord the Bible an authority in a univocal sense or understand its relation to the Church in the same way, it is still the ultimate norm for all. Mainline Protestant Churches, along with the Roman Catholic Church, also recognize that genuine dogmatic Tradition, represented by ancient creeds, councils, and confessional writings, also plays a realistic role in church life. Yet that Tradition functions not independently of the Bible, but along with it as the *norma normata*, normed by Scripture itself. But precisely as such a privileged norm, Scripture is the basic element in the Christian heritage that all Churches involved in the ecumenical movement have in common.

There are, of course, many ways of using the Bible in ecumenical endeavors. Christians of different backgrounds have learned through the Bible to pray together, to study the sacred

---

[5] For a description of this role, see pp. 78–80 above.

text together, and to use it as the motivation for common ecumenical activity together. Whereas Catholics of earlier generations worried about a generic *communicatio in sacris*, the Second Vatican Council's Decree on Ecumenism restricted that to sacramental sharing, and then with certain conditions, but recommended that Catholics in various circumstances "join in prayer with their separated brethren," as in prayer services 'for unity' and during ecumenical gatherings.[6] In fact, this has normally taken place in common services of the Word of God or Scripture Services.

The Ecumenical Institute at Bossey, near Geneva, Switzerland, has been well known for decades for its ecumenical Bible study, largely dominated by the French woman, Suzanne de Diétrich,[7] and her colleague Hendrik Kraemer.

It is, however, not just the Bible as such that has been involved in the ecumenical movement, but the adoption of the historical-critical method of interpreting the Bible by Roman Catholics in recent decades has enabled them to become deeply involved in that movement. One must remember that one of the major pre-council factors that contributed to the work of the Second Vatican Council was the encyclical of Pius XII on the promotion of biblical studies, *Divino afflante Spiritu.* That encyclical was issued during the Second World War, but it was largely responsible for the shaping of Catholic theological thinking in the period between 1945 and 1962. Even though he never used the term "historical-critical method," Pius XII urged Catholic interpreters to make a proper use of it. This meant that Catholics began to interpret the Bible as did their Protestant peers, and this did not escape the notice of their non-Catholic colleagues. Indeed, this was explicitly

---

[6] *Decree on Ecumenism* §8; cf. *Code of Canon Law* (1983), §844, 1365.
[7] See her book, *God's Unfolding Purpose: A Guide to the Study of the Bible* (Philadelphia, PA: Westminster, 1960).

noted by Lutherans, and it was one of the reasons cited by the Catholic and Lutheran "working group" that met in Strasbourg in 1965 and 1966 and paved the way for the formal international dialogue that began in 1967. That working group decided that a Study Commission was to be set up and that it should discuss "the Gospel and the Church," an explicitly biblical-theological question, because the "development of modern biblical scholarship has modified the traditional formulations of the respective positions and opened up a new approach to the confessional differences."[8] Significantly, all the biblical scholars who were chosen as members of the Study Commission were practitioners of the historical-critical method: H. Conzelmann, G. Strecker, H. Schürmann, A. Vögtle, and myself. The same has to be said of K. Stendahl and K.-H. Schelkle, who attended some sessions as consultants.

In this regard the task force that engaged in the collaborative assessment of Peter in the New Testament, eleven Protestant and Roman Catholic scholars, acknowledged in the first sentence of the book their use of "methods common in contemporary biblical criticism" and proceeded to describe the nature of New Testament writings, which "are not impartial records, but documents in which faith has shaped the presentation."[9] In using the historical-critical method in its quest for the historical Peter, the task force clearly made it its pri-

---

[8] So quoted in the Malta Report itself (§4); see H. Meyer, *Evangelium* (n. 4 above), 36. Cf. "Joint Report of the Roman Catholic/Lutheran Working Group," *Lutheran World* 13 (1966) 436–38, esp. 437.

[9] See R. E. Brown et al. (eds.), *Peter in the New Testament: A Collaborative Assessment by Protestant and Roman Catholic Scholars* (Minneapolis, MN: Augsburg; New York: Paulist, 1973) 7–8. Those involved were: P. J. Achtemeier, M. M. Bourke, P. S. Brown, R. E. Brown, J. A. Burgess, K. P. Donfried, J. A. Fitzmyer, K. Froehlich, R. H. Fuller, G. Krodel, and J. Reumann.

The same could be said of the other book, R. E. Brown et al. (eds.), *Mary in*

mary concern "to trace how the historical facts about this companion of Jesus have been developed into the New Testament portrait of the best known of the Twelve Apostles."[10] That book turned out to be so successful that it was translated into six foreign languages, Dutch, French, German, Italian, Japanese, and Spanish.[11] It thus stands as a testimony of how the Bible properly interpreted with the historical-critical method has contributed today to ecumenical endeavors. And the same would have to be said about the collaborative effort of Catholic and Protestant New Testament scholars who formed the task force that worked on the topic Mary in the New Testament.

II. *Ecumenical Translations of the Bible*

Beyond the matter of how the Bible and its interpretation have been involved in modern ecumenical endeavors there is also the question of ecumenical translations of the written Word of God. In a sense, this is nothing new, since even Je-

---

the New Testament: A Collaborative Assessment by Protestant and Roman Catholic Scholars (Philadelphia, PA: Fortress; New York: Paulist, 1978). Those involved were the same except for J. A. Burgess. Two others were added to the group: J. L. Martyn and E. H. Pagels.

[10] *Peter* (n. 9 above), 9.

[11] *Petrus in het geloof van de jonge kerk* (Boxtel: Katholieke Bijbelstiching, 1976); *Saint Pierre dans le Nouveau Testament* (LD 79; Paris: Cerf, 1974); *Der Petrus der Bibel: Eine ökumenische Untersuchung* (Stuttgart: Calwer Verlag/Katholisches Bibelwerk, 1976); *Shin-yakuseisho ni okeru Pe-te-ro* (Tokyo: Seibunsha, 1977); *Pedro en el Nuevo Testamento: Un trabajo en colaboración por autores Protestantes y Católicos* (Santander: Sal Terrae, 1976); Pietro nel Nuovo Testamento (Rome: Edizioni Borla, 1988).

Foreign translations of the book on Mary also exist: *Maria im Neuen Testament: Eine Gemeinschaftsstudie von protestantischen und römisch-katholischen Gelehrten* (Stuttgart: Katholisches Bibelwerk, 1981); *Maria nel Nuovo Testamento: Una valutazione congiunta di studiosi protestantici e cattolici* (Orizzonti biblici; Assisi: Cittadella, 1985); *Maria en el Nuevo Testamento* (Salamanca: Sigueme, 1982).

rome consulted Jewish scholars in his effort to translate the *hebraica veritas* into Latin. Yet his translation remained the work of one person.

For centuries after Jerome, Western Christians used either the Latin Vulgate or translations of the Bible made from it, until in the fifteenth and sixteenth centuries vernacular Bibles came into being. Catholics continued to use either the Vulgate or versions based on it, such as the English Douay-Rheims translation or that of Ronald Knox. Once Pius XII urged in his encyclical of 1943 that Catholics make use of the Bible in its original languages, there began the Catholic translation of Scripture from the original Hebrew, Aramaic, and Greek texts. In English that resulted in the Confraternity of Christian Doctrine version, and its successor, the New American Bible. Yet it was still a Catholic Bible.

A break with that custom came when Archbishop Gordon J. Gray of St. Andrews and Edinburgh in Scotland gave his imprimatur to a form of the RSV: *The Holy Bible: Revised Standard Version Containing the Old and New Testaments: Catholic Edition.*[12] It was called a Catholic edition because British scholars made 66 changes in the New Testament, most of them of little significance: e.g., "brethren" for "brothers"; "send her away" instead of "divorce her" (Matt 1:19); "full of grace" instead of "O favoured one" (Luke 1:28).[13] The result was that, though Catholics and Protestants were using the same English version, there was still a difference between the *form* of the RSV used by Catholics and that by Protestants.

That situation, however, changed when Richard Cardinal Cushing of Boston gave his imprimatur to *The Ox-*

---

[12] Prepared by the Catholic Biblical Association of Great Britain (London: Catholic Truth Society, 1966).

[13] See my review of the separate printing of the New Testament (Collegeville, MN: St. John's Abbey, 1965), *TS* 26 (1975) 672–75.

ford *Annotated Bible with the Apocrypha: Revised Standard Version.*[14] Cushing was dependent on more enlightened advisors (P. J. King, W. Van Etten Casey, and E. H. Maly), and no changes were made in the text of either the Old or the New Testament of the RSV in this Oxford annotated edition.[15] At length, English-speaking Catholics could read the same text of the Bible as their Protestant neighbors. This was obviously of lasting effect and significant ecumenical value, but it meant that Catholics were, in fact, using a Protestant Bible. Even though, after the Second Vatican Council, Catholics were taken onto the translation board of the Standard Bible, myself included for several years, the RSV and the NRSV have remained the modern revisions of the renowned Protestant Authorized Version of 1611, commonly called the King James Version. This form of the Bible has appeared in various "Common Bibles," which order the books differently and even admit the title "Deuterocanonical" for various books among those that were earlier called in the tradition the "Apocrypha." But there is as yet no English ecumenical translation of the Bible.

Such a translation does exist in other modern languages. For instance, there is the justly famous *Traduction oecuménique de la Bible,*[16] on which French Catholic and Protestant biblical scholars worked together. It is also an annotated version, which has sought in its notes to strike a balance between confessional differences in interpretation.

Similarly, in German there is *Die Bibel: Einheitsübersetzung der Heiligen Schrift, Altes und Neues Testament.*[17]

---

[14] Ed. H. G. May and B. M. Metzger (New York: Oxford University, 1965).

[15] See my review, *TS* 28 (1967) 173.

[16] Edition intégrale in 2 vols.; ed. J. Potin (Paris: Cerf/Les Bergers et les Mages, 1975; repr. 1985).

[17] Ed. O. Knoch et al. (Stuttgart: Katholisches Bibelanstalt/Deutsche Bibelstiftung, 1979–80).

The latest form of it is a revision of a joint Protestant-Catholic translation first launched in 1962, and it has been approved by the episcopal conferences of Germany, Austria, Switzerland, Luxemburg, and Liège, as well as by the Council of the Evangelische Kirche in Deutschland.

Less successful has been the Italian counterpart of these ecumenical translations. It is *La Bibbia concordata: Tradotta dai testi originali, con introduzione e note.*[18] It is the work of Catholic, Jewish, Orthodox, and Protestant members of the Società Biblica Italiana, but it is uneven in its results and has been no little criticized.

In the instance of these ecumenical translations of the Bible one sees how Scripture itself has become the ecumenical bridge. In these instances the best of Protestant and Catholic biblical scholars have usually cooperated, and the projects represent a form of common and united work that would have been unthinkable in earlier centuries and decades.

III. *Scripture in the Catholic-Lutheran Dialogue in the United States*

I come now to the role that Scripture itself has played in a concrete ecumenical situation, viz. in the national dialogue between Lutherans and Catholics in the United States. The idea of a national dialogue originated in the 1960s and came from Dr. Paul C. Empie, then the executive director of the national Lutheran Council in New York. He consulted Bishop (later Cardinal) John Wright of Pittsburgh and Lawrence Cardinal Shehan of Baltimore about the possibility of Catholic and Lutheran theologians engaging in serious discus-

---

[18] Ed. S. Cipriani et al. (Milan: Mondadori, 1968).

sion and debate over the issues that had divided the two church-bodies since the sixteenth century.

The upshot of Empie's consultation was a meeting of eight Lutheran and nine Catholic theologians in Baltimore in July 1965. The topic chosen for that first round of discussion was the Status of the Nicene Creed as Dogma of the Church, an issue removed from Scripture as well as from neuralgic, divisive areas of controversy. It was deliberately chosen as a topic on which there would be little disagreement in order to break the ice, to get the discussions started on a more or less neutral matter of common concern. In the brief two-page Summary Statement, issued as the result of this first consultation,[19] both sides agreed that "the Nicene Faith, grounded in the biblical proclamation about Christ and the trinitarian baptismal formulas used in the Church, is both doxology to God the Father and dogma about God the Son." They also acknowledged that

> different understandings of the movement from kerygma to dogma obtain in the two communities. Full inquiry must therefore be made into two topics: first, the nature and structure of the teaching authority in the Church; and, secondly, the role of Scripture in relation to the teaching office of the Church.[20]

In 1966 the dialogue continued in round two on another

---

[19] *The Status of the Nicene Creed as Dogma of the Church* (Published jointly by representatives of the U. S. A. National Committee of the Lutheran World Federation and the Bishops' Commission for Ecumenical Affairs, 1965) 31–32. The statement can also be found in *Building Unity: Ecumenical Dialogues with Roman Catholic Participation in the United States* (Ecumenical Documents IV; ed. J. A. Burgess and J. Gros; New York/Mahwah, NJ: Paulist, 1989) 88–89.

[20] *The Status*, 32. These topics were later taken up in the sixth and ninth rounds of the dialogue: Teaching Authority & Infallibility in the Church; and The Word of God: Scripture and Tradition.

topic that was thought to be equally noncontroversial, One Baptism for the Remission of Sins. A very brief Joint Statement, signed by the two co-chairmen, Bp. T. Austin Murphy and Dr. Paul C. Empie, was issued along with the texts of four position papers.[21] The Joint Statement admitted that "although we use the same words with somewhat different meanings, we also upon occasion have different ways of saying the same things." Yet Lutheran systematic theologian Warren A. Quanbeck, who had been an observer at the Second Vatican Council in Rome and who had to react to the biblical papers on the topic prepared by Raymond E. Brown and Krister Stendahl, recognized that they "came to substantial agreement on what the New Testament says about baptism."[22] Thus the interpretation of New Testament passages on baptism by a Catholic and a Lutheran manifested agreement and made its contribution to ecumenism. Once again, one has to note that both of these papers were interpretations of the New Testament data according to the historical-critical method.

The third round of discussions, undertaken in 1967, was devoted to the Eucharist as Sacrifice, a topic that one might have thought would be controversial because of historic differences on the matter between the two traditions since the sixteenth century. Three papers were presented and discussed on biblical aspects of the topic: "The Eucharist as Sacrifice in the New Testament" and "The Words of Institution," both by the Lutheran New Testament scholar and now Bishop in

---

[21] *One Baptism for the Remission of Sins* (ed. P. C. Empie and W. W. Baum; New York: National Lutheran Council, 1966; Washington, DC: N.C.W.C., 1967) 85. Also in *Building Unity*, 90.

[22] *One Baptism*, 72. Catholic J. W. Baker commented similarly: "There was no disagreement on the biblical presentations" (p. 80).

Sweden, Bertil E. Gärtner, and "Propitiation," by the Catholic scholar, Jerome D. Quinn. Thus the scriptural basis of the matter was duly handled. When the Common Statement on the matter was issued, it noted a remarkable "growing consensus" on the Lord's Supper between the two groups:[23] "Lutherans and Roman Catholics alike acknowledge that in the Lord's supper 'Christ is present as the Crucified who died for our sins and who rose again for our justification, as the once-for-all sacrifice for the sins of the world who gives himself to the faithful.' "[24] And "we affirm that in the sacrament of the Lord's supper Jesus Christ, true God and true man, is present wholly and entirely, in his body and blood, under the signs of bread and wine."[25] As remarkable as this sounds, there was also a noteworthy clarification of what Catholics understand today by "offering Christ," and although there was not complete agreement about transsubstantiation or the offering of the sacrifice "for the living and the dead," these issues were considered not to stand as obstacles to the basic agreement. Here the degree of unanimity was unexpected.

A truly controversial topic, however, was taken up in the fourth round of the dialogue and debated from 1968 to 1970, Eucharist and Ministry. It dealt with the controversial matter of the validity of Lutheran orders. In this case, only one explicitly biblical paper was discussed, "Ministry in the New Testament," prepared by J. D. Quinn, a Roman Catholic. But in the statement of Common Observations on Eucharistic Ministry, paragraphs 7–11 dealt with the pertinent biblical

---

[23] *The Eucharist as Sacrifice* (Lutherans and Catholics in Dialogue 3; New York: National Committee of the Lutheran World Federation; Washington, DC: N.C.W.C., 1967) 187. Also in *Building Unity*, 91–101.

[24] *Eucharist as Sacrifice* (n. 23 above), 188.

[25] Ibid., 192.

material: ministry in the context of God's act in Christ, ministry of the people of God, and the special Ministry.[26] But the topic itself involved many more issues associated with the tradition that had grown out of such New Testament data, and most of the discussion was centered on them, many of which were of divisive nature. This fourth round in the dialogue on Eucharist and Ministry has proved to be the one most controverted; at times it has been especially criticized.[27]

Still more controversial was the topic taken up in the fifth round from 1970 to 1973, for the dialogue had finally come to the neuralgic question of the papacy, Papal Primacy and the Universal Church. In this round the biblical data entered more fully into the discussion than in previous rounds and made a contribution that was truly telling. Yet when one looks for an explicitly biblical position paper in the volume finally

---

[26] *Eucharist and Ministry* (Lutherans and Catholics in Dialogue 4; New York: National Committee of the Lutheran World Federation; Washington, DC: N.C.W.C., 1970) 7–33, esp. 9–10. Also in *Building Unity*, 102–24.

[27] Especially the boldface paragraph toward the end of the reflections of the Catholic participants. It reads:

> As Roman Catholic theologians, we acknowledge in the spirit of Vatican II that the Lutheran communities with which we have been in dialogue are truly Christian churches, possessing the elements of holiness and truth that mark them as organs of grace and salvation. Furthermore, in our study we have found serious defects in the arguments customarily used against the validity of the eucharistic Ministry of the Lutheran churches. In fact, we see no persuasive reason to deny the possibility of the Roman Catholic church recognizing the validity of this Ministry. Accordingly we ask the authorities of the Roman Catholic church whether the ecumenical urgency flowing from Christ's will for unity may not dictate that the Roman Catholic church recognize the validity of the Lutheran Ministry and, correspondingly, the presence of the body and blood of Christ in the eucharistic celebrations of the Lutheran churches (*Eucharist and Ministry*, 31–32).

published, there is none.[28] But a statement in the volume about procedures explains the relation of the special work of the subsidiary task force, which published *Peter in the New Testament*, to the dialogue proper.[29] That task force, consisting of eleven New Testament scholars, had met fifteen times, from October 1971 to March 1973, and studied every passage in the New Testament relating to Peter. The results of that collaborative study were taken up by the dialogue members and are duly summarized in paragraphs 9–13 of the Common Statement.[30] There one finds a recognition of the limited information in the New Testament about the historical career of Simon Peter, of different aspects or images of Ministry associated with him in reference to the Church as a whole, and various descriptions of his role and career. One also notes there "the thrust" involved in such images, "a trajectory" of them as they develop from earlier to later images. Such a development "does not constitute papacy in its later technical sense, but one can see the possibility of an orientation in that direction."[31] Hence, in this instance the New Testament data, critically assessed, have been seen to contribute in a remarkable way to what the document calls "the Petrine function" in the Christian Church:

> Although we are aware of the danger of attributing to the church in New Testament times a modern style or model of universality, we have found it appropriate to speak of a Petrine function, using this term to describe *a particular*

---

[28] *Papal Primacy and the Universal Church* (Lutherans and Catholics in Dialogue 5; ed. P. C. Empie and T. A. Murphy; Minneapolis, MN: Augsburg, 1974). The common statement and the Lutheran and Catholic reflections are found on pp. 9–38; also in *Building Unity*, 125–59.

[29] See nn. 9 and 11 above.

[30] *Papal Primacy* (n. 28 above), 13–16.

[31] Ibid., 15–16.

> *form of Ministry exercised by a person, officeholder, or lo-*
> *cal church with reference to the church as a whole.*[32]

This recognition of a Petrine function in the Christian church, which has grown out of the New Testament data, is a noteworthy advance in ecumenism, and especially in the debate about the papacy and its function in the church.

The sixth round was devoted to an equally controversial aspect of the papacy, Teaching Authority and Infallibility in the Church, debated from 1973 to 1978. This topic is intimately related to that of the fifth round, papal primacy, but it was separated from it because of the special problems related to papal teaching authority,[33] and one aspect of the papacy had to be discussed at a time. Among the 26 position-papers prepared and discussed in this lengthy round, four were devoted to biblical aspects of the matter. Two treated the office of teaching in the Christian Church according to the New Testament, one by a Roman Catholic, myself, and a response by Lutheran J. Reumann; two others were written by J. D. Quinn, on the biblical *loci* pertaining to infallibility and on the terminology of faith, truth, teaching, and the Spirit in the Pastoral Letters. Again, in this instance the New Testament data were limited, and most of the time was rather spent in this lengthy round on the philosophical nature of language and utterances and the possibility of infallible statements, on the history of the dogma of infallibility, and on the papal exercise of infallibility in the definition of two Marian dogmas, the Immaculate Conception (1854) and the Assumption

---

[32] Ibid., 11 (§4). The italics are used in the original.

[33] *Teaching Authority & Infallibility in the Church* (Lutherans and Catholics in Dialogue 6; ed. P. C. Empie, T. A. Murphy, and J. A. Burgess; Minneapolis, MN: Augsburg, 1980). The common statement and the reflection papers are found on pp. 11–68. Also in *Building Unity*, 160–216.

(1950). However, the Common Statement did incorporate a fresh look at the biblical data, which was devoted to the treatment of Jesus Christ as authority, the gospel and its authority, especially as proclaimed by witnesses, recorded in the New Testament, summarized in *regulae fidei*, served by Ministers, and made alive by the work of the Spirit. What was remarkable in this round was the list of eleven points of convergence agreed to by both sides. There is even one admitting the perpetuity of the church and "its indefectibility, i.e. its perseverance in the truth of the gospel, in its mission, and in its life of faith," and another about "Ministries and structures charged with the teaching of Christian doctrine and with supervision and coordination of the ministry of the whole people of God": that "their task includes the mandate for bishops or other leaders to 'judge doctrine and condemn doctrine that is contrary to the Gospel.' "[34] And yet among the eleven points of convergence "infallibility" never appears. That term does not occur in the Bible, and its use in traditional theology is different from the inerrancy of the Bible, an issue that had to be clarified in the course of the discussions of this round.

Scripture played a still more important role in the seventh round of the dialogue, which from 1978 until 1983 was devoted to Justification by Faith. Here the national dialogue finally came to *the* Reformation topic. Whereas I, as a Roman Catholic, had been given the task of presenting the New Testament data on the office of teaching in the Christian Church in round six, J. Reumann, a Lutheran New Testament scholar, was assigned the task of summarizing the biblical data on this important topic in this round. Although the New Testament data alone on this topic are far more numerous than those on Peter, so that they might have been assigned to a

---

[34] *Teaching Authority* (n. 33 above), 31.

similar subsidiary task force for study and analysis, it was not done so in this case. It was rather thought that the biblical material was so important to this round of discussion that the whole dialogue team had to engage in the common discussion of it. The result was that Reumann's presentation stretched over three semi-annual sessions (1980–1981), and both J. D. Quinn and myself had to respond to his presentation. Comments from the Lutheran side were also made by J. A. Burgess. The bulk of the material that Reumann presented was such that it could not all be used in the common statement to be prepared. So it was decided that he should publish it separately. This he did in *"Righteousness" in the New Testament: "Justification" in the United States Lutheran-Roman Catholic Dialogue.*[35]

When one examines the official publication of round seven, *Justification by Faith,*[36] one can see how the biblical material played a major role in the discussions of this round. It is not used in the history of the question (part I), where it might have been expected, but rather as the first section in part III, Perspectives for Reconstruction (§§122–49). The reasons for such a use of the biblical material were many, but one major factor was that "in recent decades developments in the study of Scripture have brought Catholics and Lutherans to a fuller agreement about the meaning of many passages controverted at least since the sixteenth century."[37] For instance, one notes the shift in the interpretation of "the righteousness of

God" and of "justification" in modern New Testament study: "Recent biblical scholarship sees the righteousness of which Paul speaks both as a gift from God and, in some passages, as an attribute or quality of God, a power exercised on behalf of sinful humanity to save and justify (*heilsetzende Macht*). This widespread consensus in the modern understanding of *dikaiosyne theou*, according to which it is an attribute, but also his power present to his gift, should help us to go beyond the divisive issues of the sixteenth century."[38] Finally, what is particularly remarkable about this document is the "Declaration" with which it closes (§§161–64), too lengthy to quote here in full, but which ends with the significant sentence, "We believe that we have reached such a consensus."

The one area in which the Catholic and Lutheran participants did not fully agree was on the idea of justification by faith as a criteriological principle, i.e., that it is the *articulus stantis et cadentis ecclesiae*, "the article by which the church stands or falls." This is an article of Lutheran systematic theology, which maintains that all Church life, practices, and preaching must be normed and governed by the article of justification by faith. As such, this criteriological use of justification by faith is not found in the New Testament. It may be regarded as a theological extension of the biblical teaching, an example of a Lutheran *norma normata*. There is certainly a sense in which the principle would be acknowledged by Catholics, viz., that all Church life, practices, and preaching have to be normed by the gospel, but the Catholic members hesitated to identify that gospel solely with justification by faith.[39]

In any case, this criteriological aspect of justification led to the choice of the topic for the eighth round of the dialogue,

---

[38] Ibid., 60–61 (§131).
[39] See C. J. Peter, "Justification by Faith and the Need of Another Critical Principle," ibid., 304–15.

which during the years 1983–1990 treated the One Mediator, the Saints, and Mary. This was the round of longest duration and dealt with issues that were not as basic as justification by faith, but that have in reality caused more division than anything else ever since the appearance of the *Augsburg Confession* (1530). The book that was published as a result of this eighth round of dialogue contains the Common Statement and Catholic and Lutheran reflection papers.[40] Out of 43 position papers prepared and discussed in this round, three treated biblical topics: J. Reumann's paper on "How Do We Interpret 1 Timothy 2:1–5?"; J. A. Burgess's "Three Reflections"; and my own paper, "Biblical Data on the Veneration, Intercession, and Invocation of Holy People."

This may seem minimal, but once again one must recall the work of the subsidiary task force that produced *Mary in the New Testament*.[41] Since the New Testament data on Mary had been prepared separately, my own position paper concentrated on the saints or holy people. The results of the task force's work were summarized by Reumann and myself and were used in the second part of the common statement, Biblical and Historical Foundations, esp. in paragraphs 143–55. But the summary of those results caused some problems, because some Catholic members of the dialogue objected to the treatment of New Testament passages about Mary that seemed to them too negatively interpreted (Mark 3:20–35; Matt 13:53–58; and John 2:1–11).[42] In this case, it was the reluctance of systematic theologians to accept the interpreta-

---

[40] *The One Mediator, the Saints, and Mary* (Lutherans and Catholics in Dialogue 8; ed. H. G. Anderson, J. F. Stafford, and J. A. Burgess; Minneapolis, MN: Augsburg, 1992) 19–115 (common statement), 117–24 (Catholic reflections), 125–32 (Lutheran reflections).

[41] See nn. 9 and 11 above.

[42] Compare, for instance, §§143–55 with corresponding passages in *Mary in the New Testament*.

tion of their biblical colleagues. It was not a confessional difference between Lutheran and Catholic exegetes, but a difference between Catholic systematic theologians and exegetes in general, and it brought home to us that systematicians still prefer to do exegesis as it was done in the good old days.

One issue that emerged prominently in this round was the question of the "theological extension" of the meaning of biblical passages. For instance, a New Testament passage that was important for the topic was 1 Tim 2:1–6, which reads:

> First of all, then, I ask that supplications, prayers, petitions, and thanksgivings be offered for everyone, for kings and for all in authority, that we may lead a quiet and tranquil life in all devotion and dignity. This is good and pleasing to God our savior, who wills everyone to be saved and to come to the knowledge of the truth. For there is one God. There is also one mediator between God and the human race, Christ Jesus, himself human, who gave himself as ransom for all.

Here the author asserts, "There is one God. There is also one mediator between God and human beings, Jesus Christ, himself human, who gave himself as a ransom for all" (vv. 5–6). This is a clear affirmation of the unique mediation of Christ Jesus, a verse that figures prominently in the *Augsburg Confession* (§ 21), on "the Cult of the Saints." In the immediately preceding verses of the same paragraph or context, however, the author urges that "supplications, prayers, petitions, and thanksgivings be offered for everyone, for kings and all in authority" (vv. 1–2). Clearly, the author was addressing persons still in this life (living saints), urging them to address prayers to God on behalf of other living human beings. Moreover, he saw no conflict between such intercession for others and his own teaching about the unique mediation of Jesus Christ.

Hence the question had to be asked: How legitimate would it be to extend theologically the author's recommendation of supplications and prayers for others to persons who have died (deceased saints)? Could not the invocation of departed saints (that they pray for all of us) be considered a theological extension of 1 Tim 2:1–2? This was treated in my paper, and an answer from the Lutheran side came in Reumann's paper.

This question of the theological extension of the meaning of biblical passages touched on an issue that had surfaced many times in all the rounds of dialogue since 1965, but had never been adequately dealt with. For "theological extension" is one way of explaining the growth and development of a tradition related to and rooted in Scripture. Hence the topic for the ninth round of dialogue became Scripture and Tradition, a topic that was mentioned in the first round of dialogue in 1965, and to which the national dialogue came only in 1990. The topic was debated from 1990–1992. The common statement on it will appear in a forthcoming booklet to be entitled *The Word of God: Scripture and Tradition*.[43] In this case, Scripture is one of the two main foci. At issue is the relation of the two elements, Scripture and Tradition, to each other and to "the Word of God," properly understood. For Roman Catholics the topic touches on whether Scripture and Tradition form one or two fonts of revelation, and for Lutherans it touches on the sense of *sola Scriptura*, and the problem that the ancient Creeds and their Confessional Books create with reference to it.

From this rapid survey one can see that Scripture has indeed played a major role as a bridge in one area of modern ecumenism. It is clear that, if the attitude toward the Bible and its interpretation had not changed in the Catholic Church

---

[43] (Lutherans and Catholics in Dialogue 9; Minneapolis, MN: Augsburg, 1994).

since the encyclical of Pius XII in 1943, there would undoubtedly have been no Second Vatican Council, no Decree on Ecumenism, and no bilateral consultations. For the dialogue with the Lutherans, both on the international level and on the national level in the United States, was furthered precisely by the prominence that the Bible had assumed in Roman Catholic life in the middle of the twentieth century. And this is but one example of an ecumenical dialogue in which the Catholic Church has been involved. Even though the Lutheran-Catholic dialogue has taken up more controversial issues than other bilateral consultations, and more that have been closely related to Scripture, other consultations have also touched at times on biblical issues.[44]

This survey, then, serves to illustrate how Scripture has indeed served as a bridge in ecumenism in the latter part of the twentieth century. That ecumenical movement will continue beyond the end of this century, and Scripture is sure to play a major role in its continuing development.

---

[44] See further J. Reumann and J. A. Fitzmyer, "Scripture as Norm for Our Common Faith," *Journal of Ecumenical Studies* 30 (1993–94) 81–107.

1. BIBLICAL INDEX

2. TOPICAL INDEX

3. MODERN AUTHORS

OTHER BOOKS BY JOSEPH A. FITZMYER, S.J.
PUBLISHED BY PAULIST PRESS

According to Paul
A Christological Catechism (New Revised and
   Expanded Edition)
Luke the Theologian
Mary in the New Testament
Responses to 101 Questions on the Dead Sea Scrolls
Scripture and Christology